I0476463

Creative Garden Coloring Book:

Art of Nature as a Stress Relief Therapy

Will Nehmen

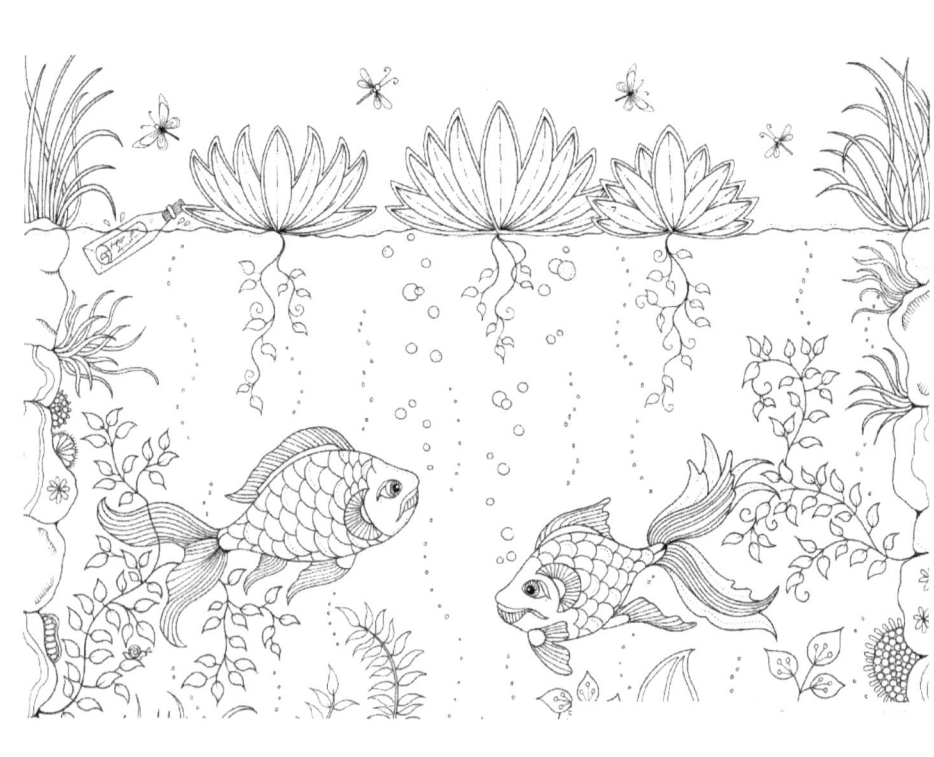

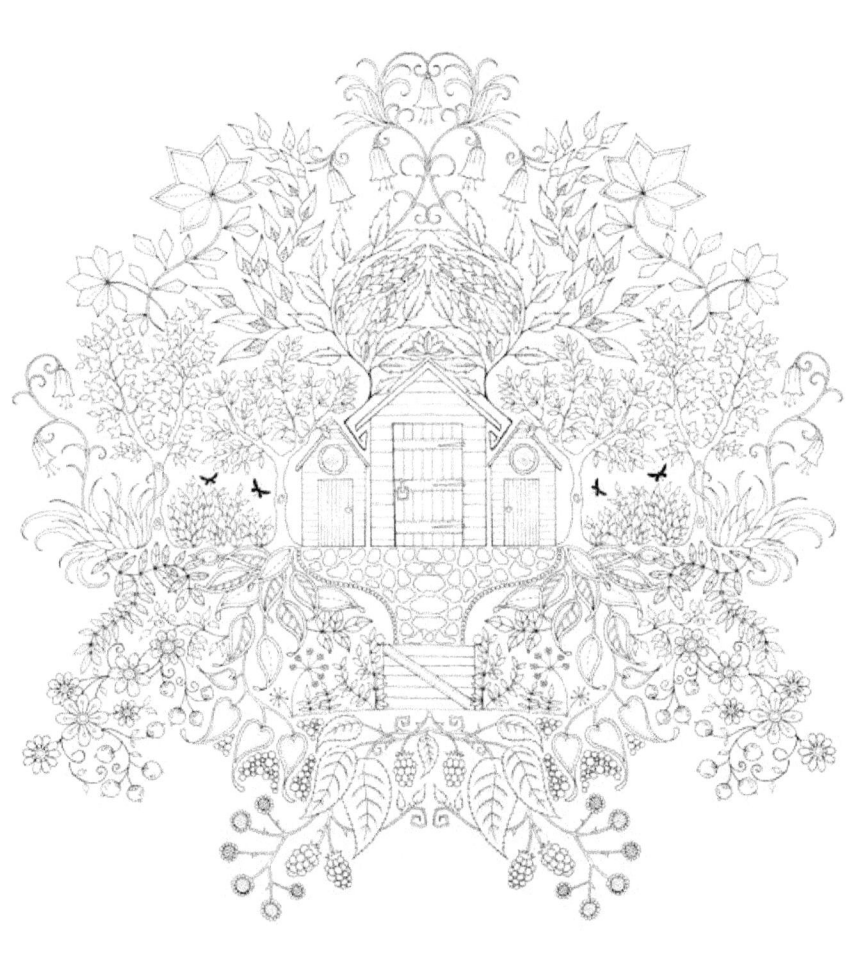

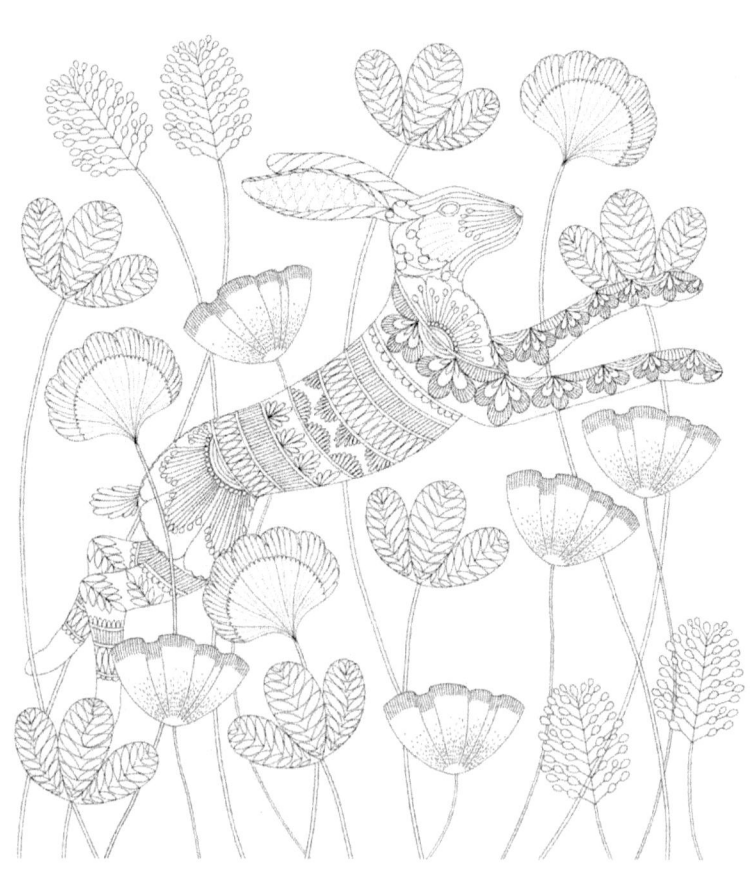

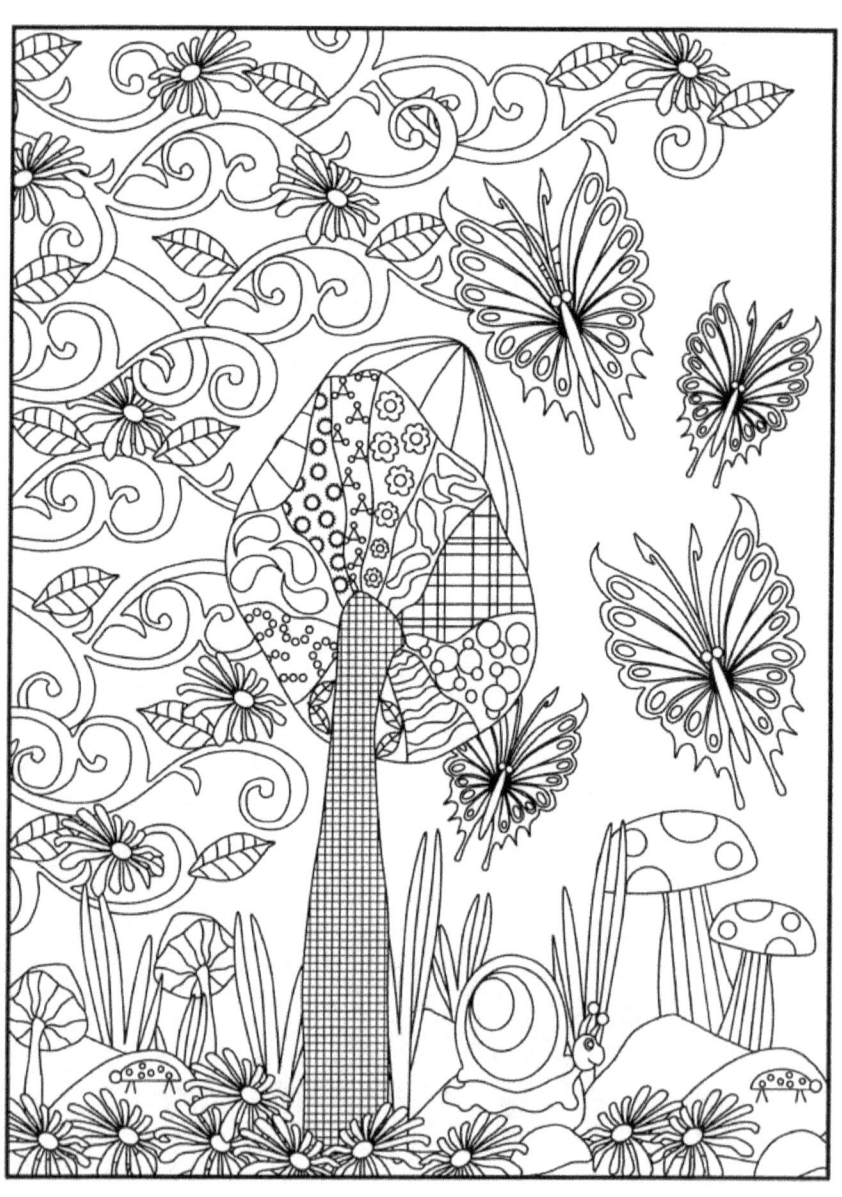

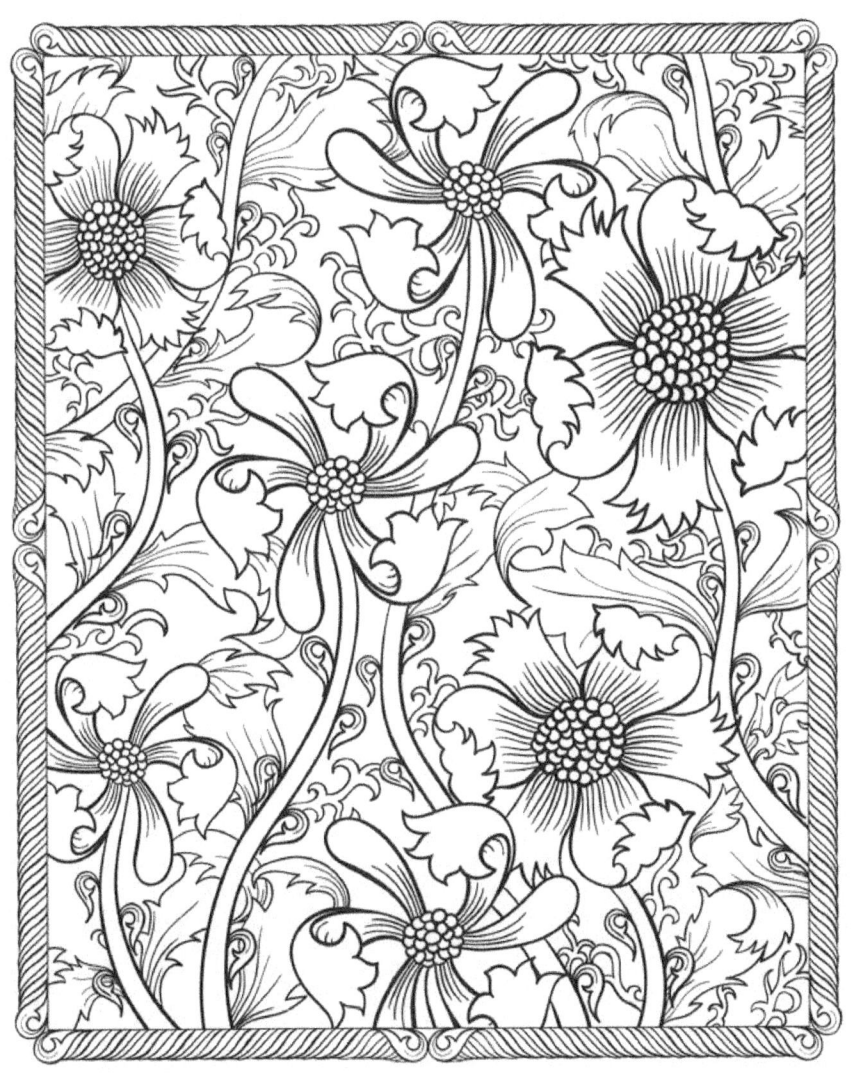

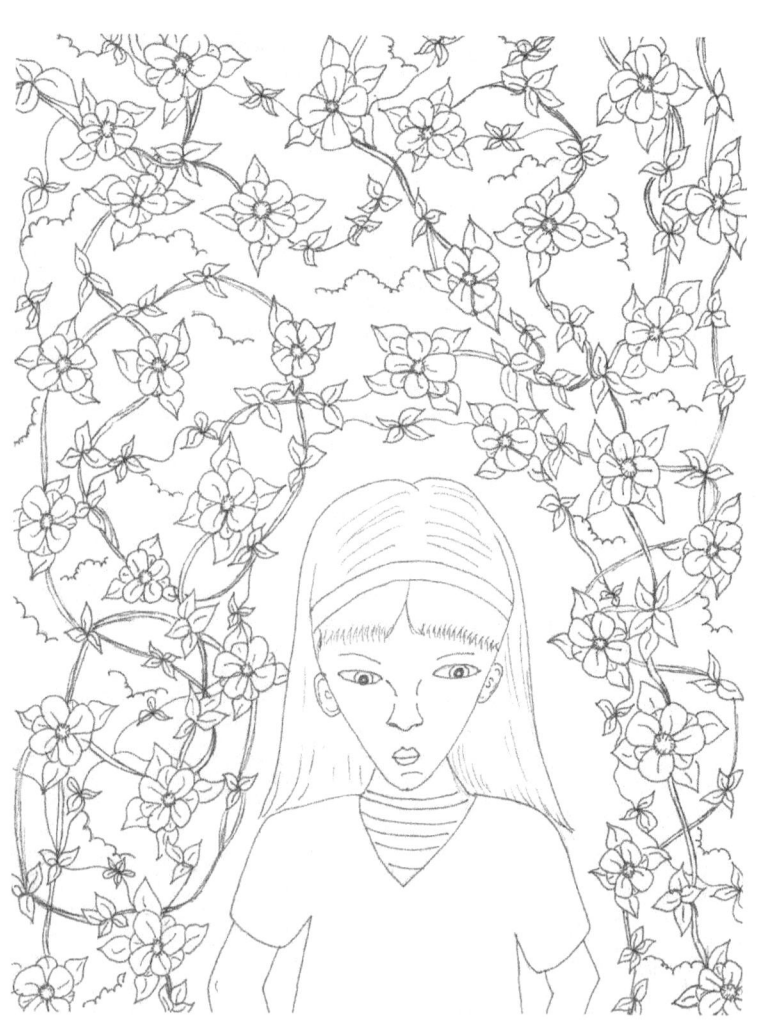

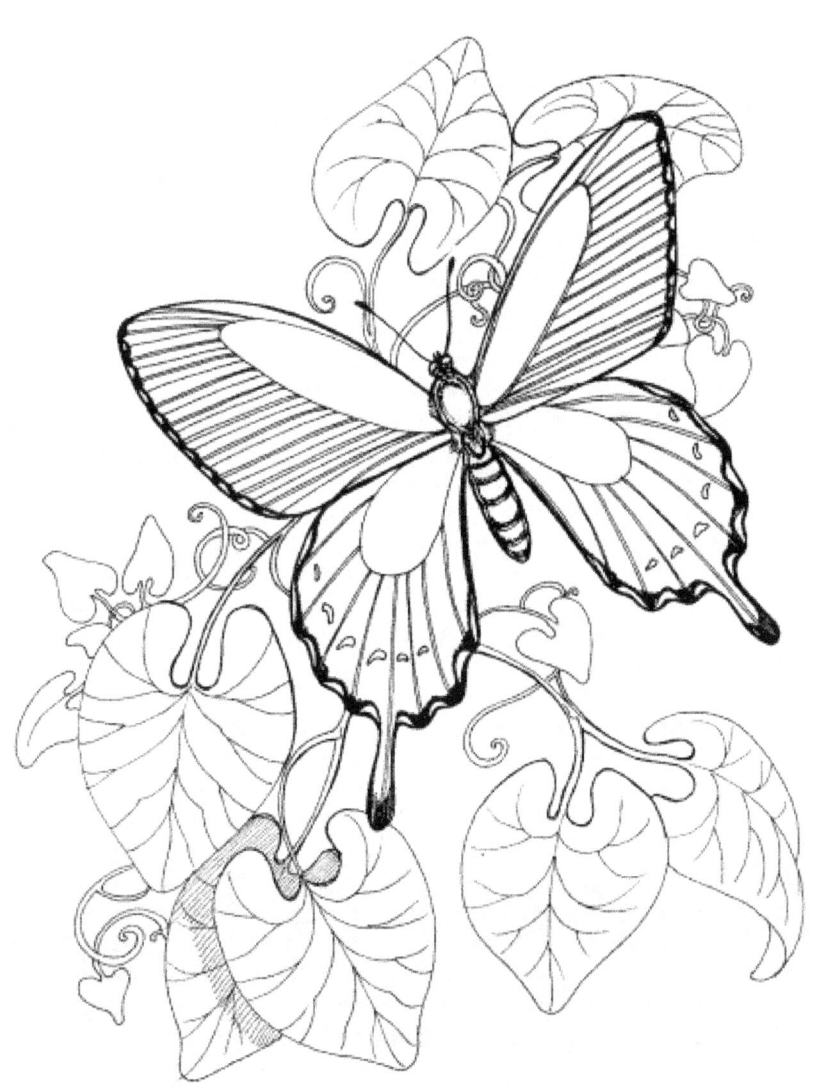

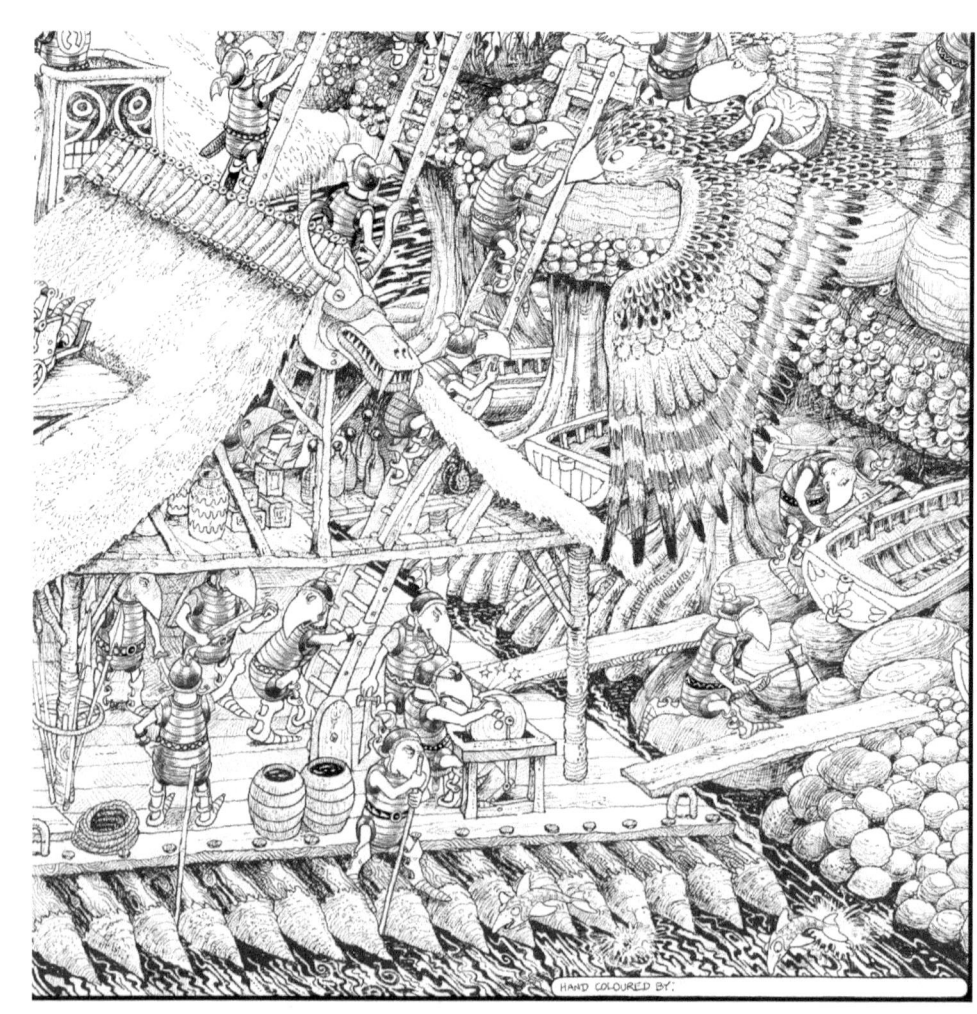

HAND COLOURED BY:

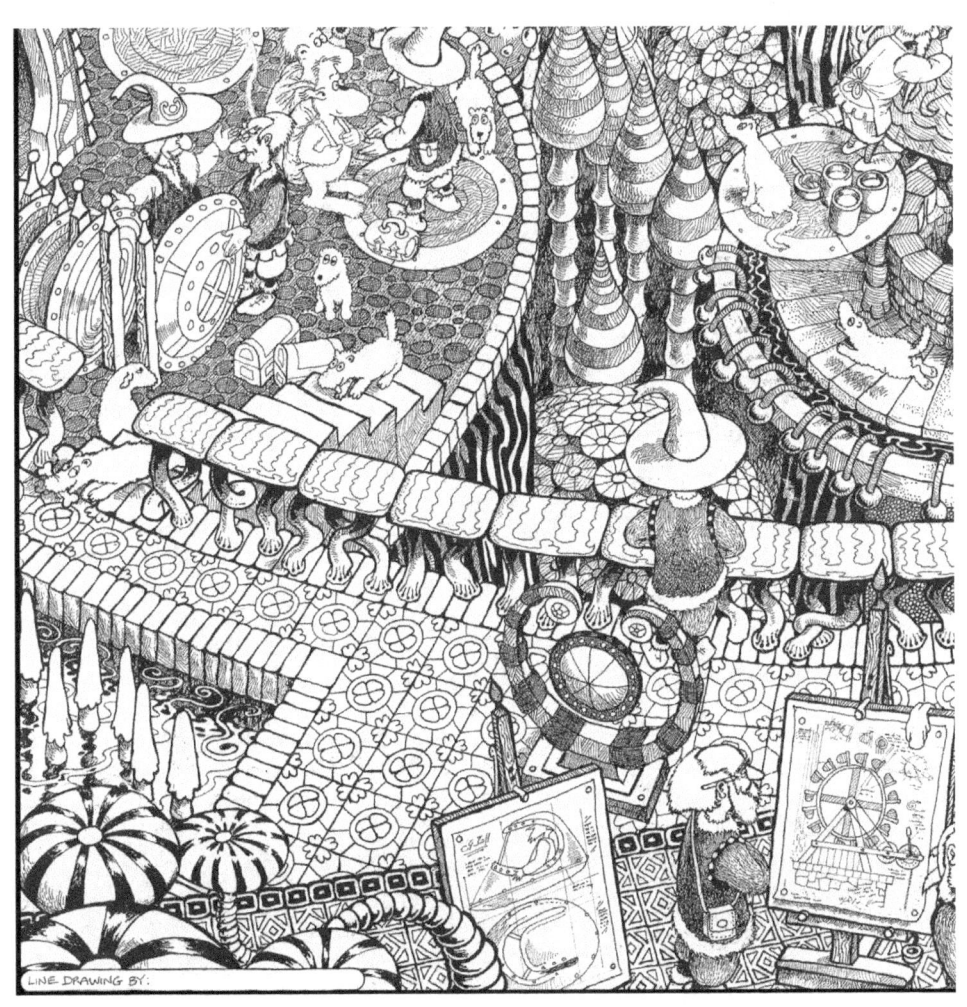

LINE DRAWING BY:

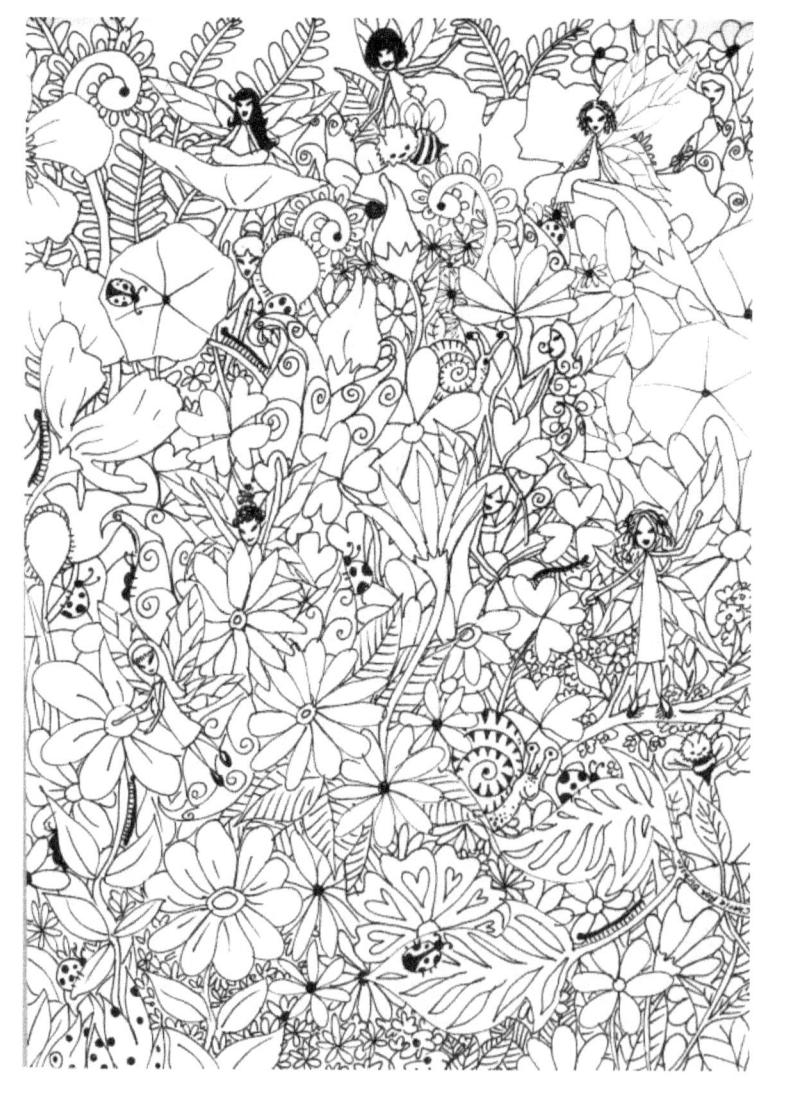

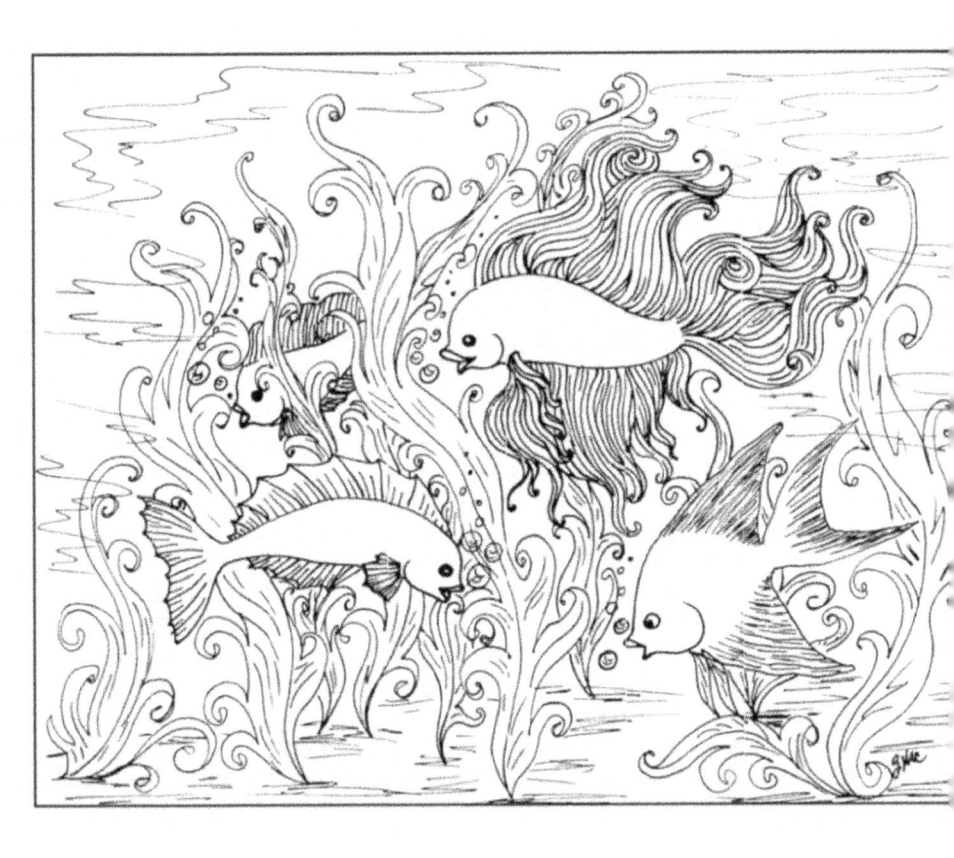

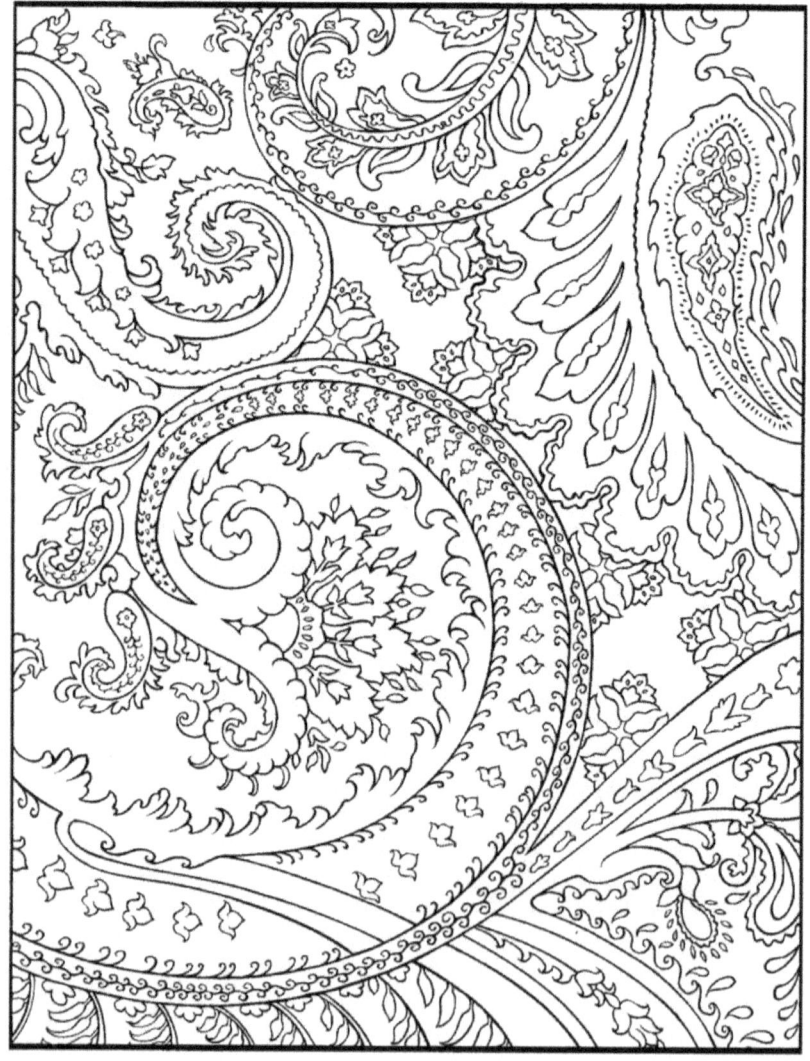

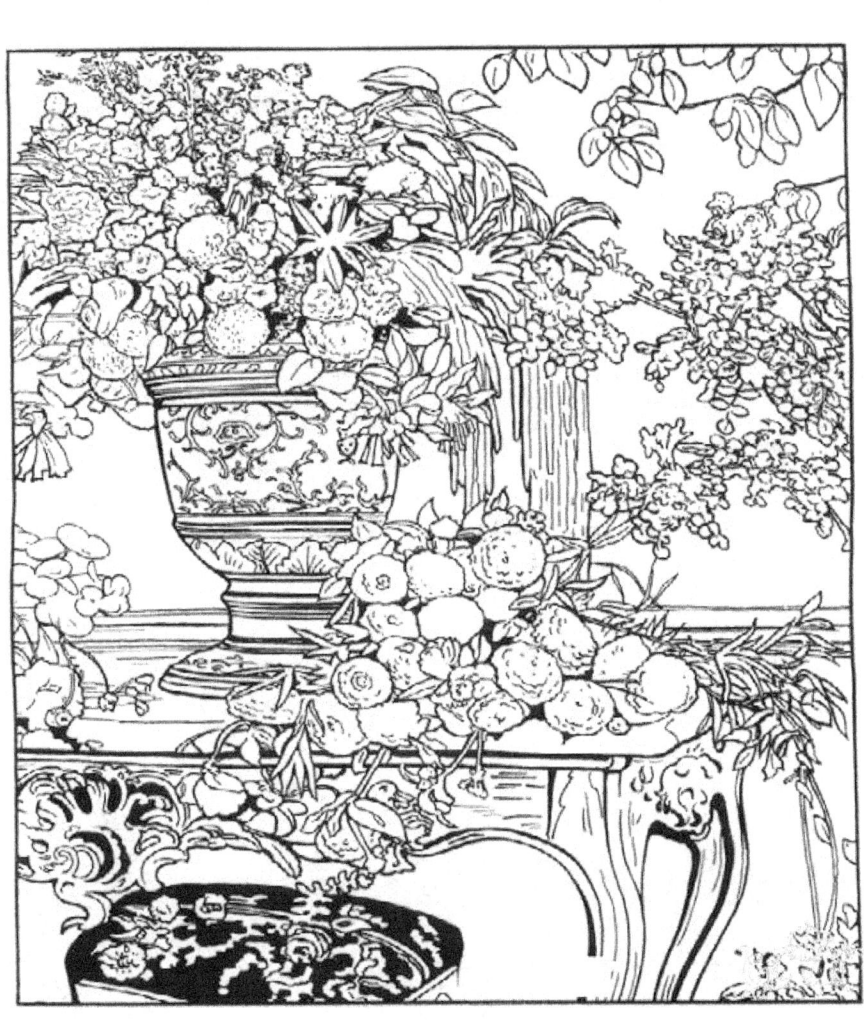

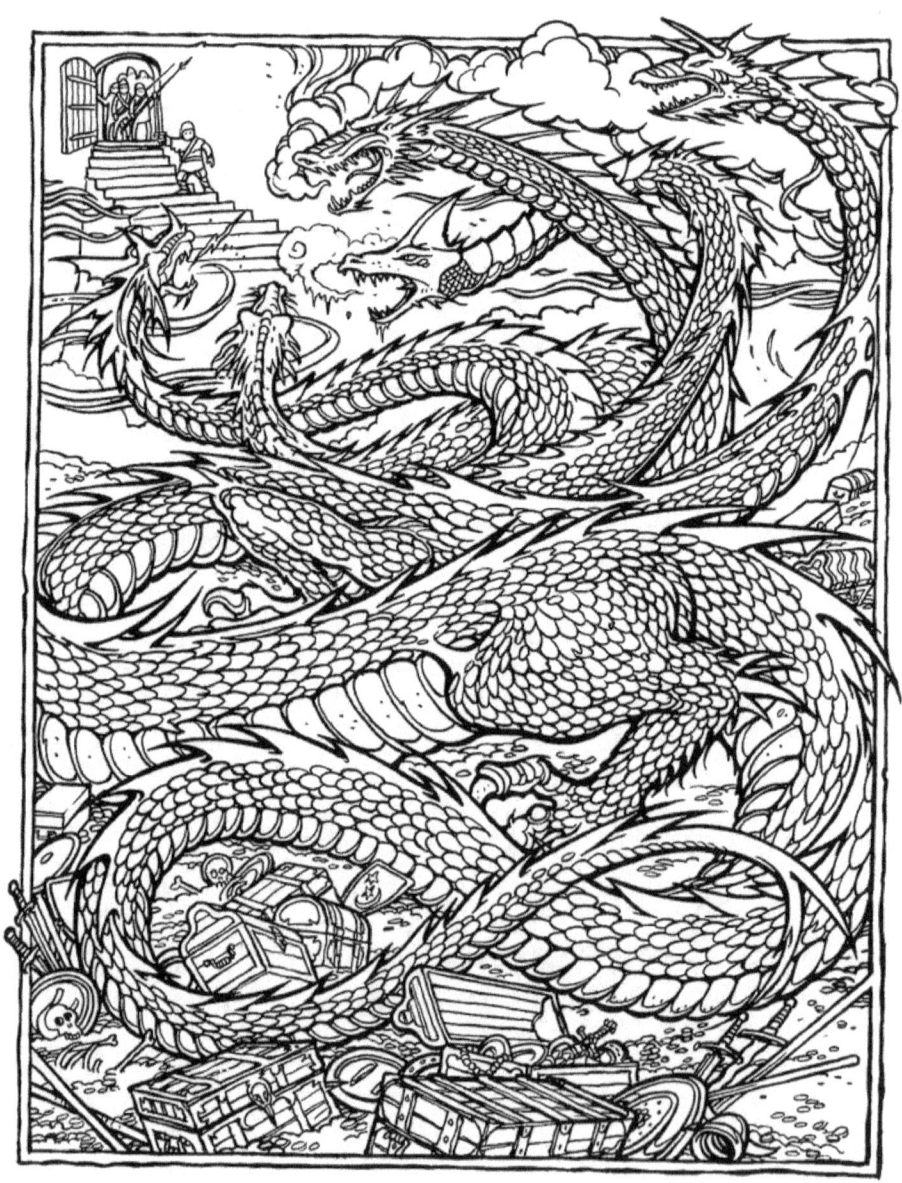

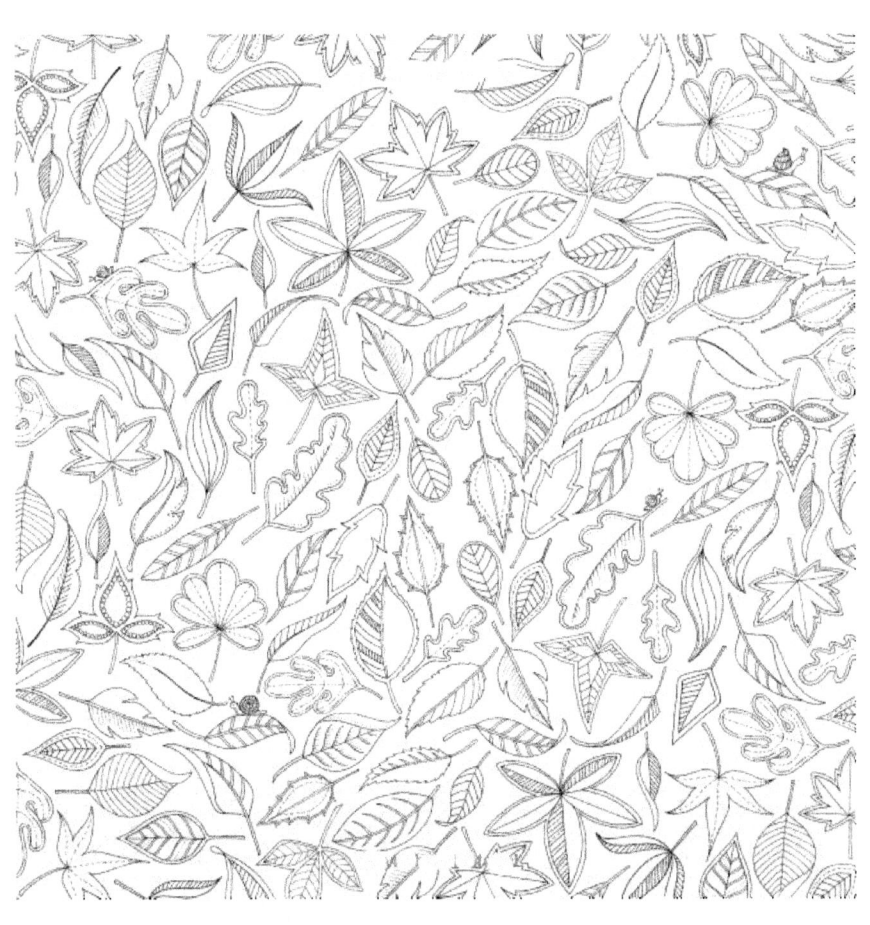

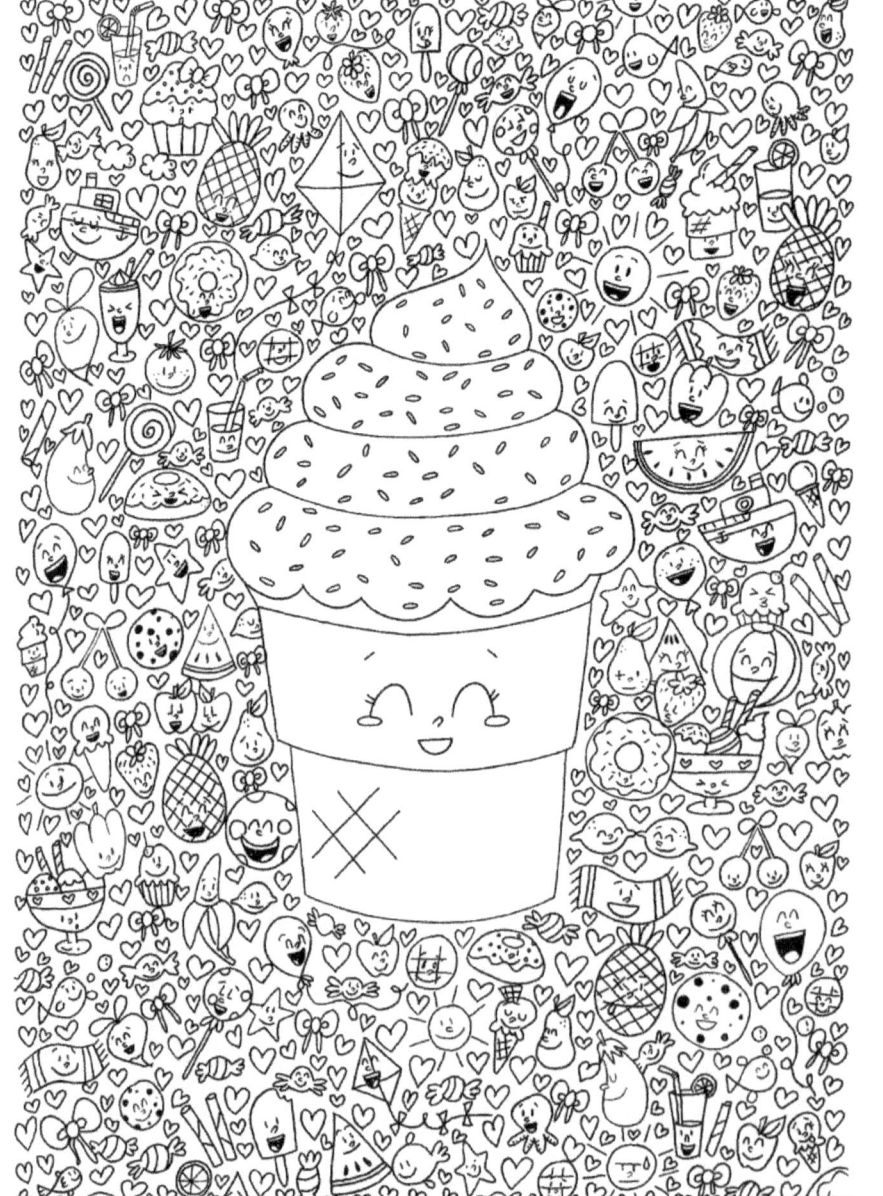

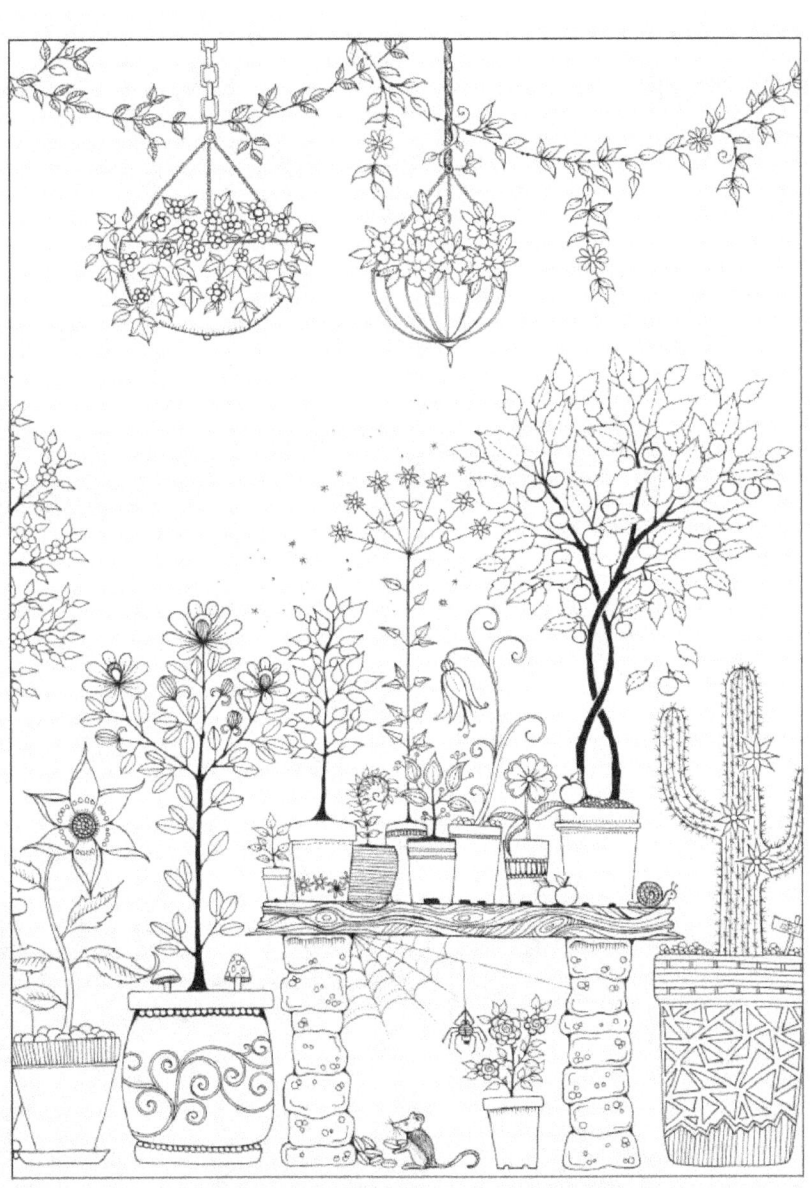

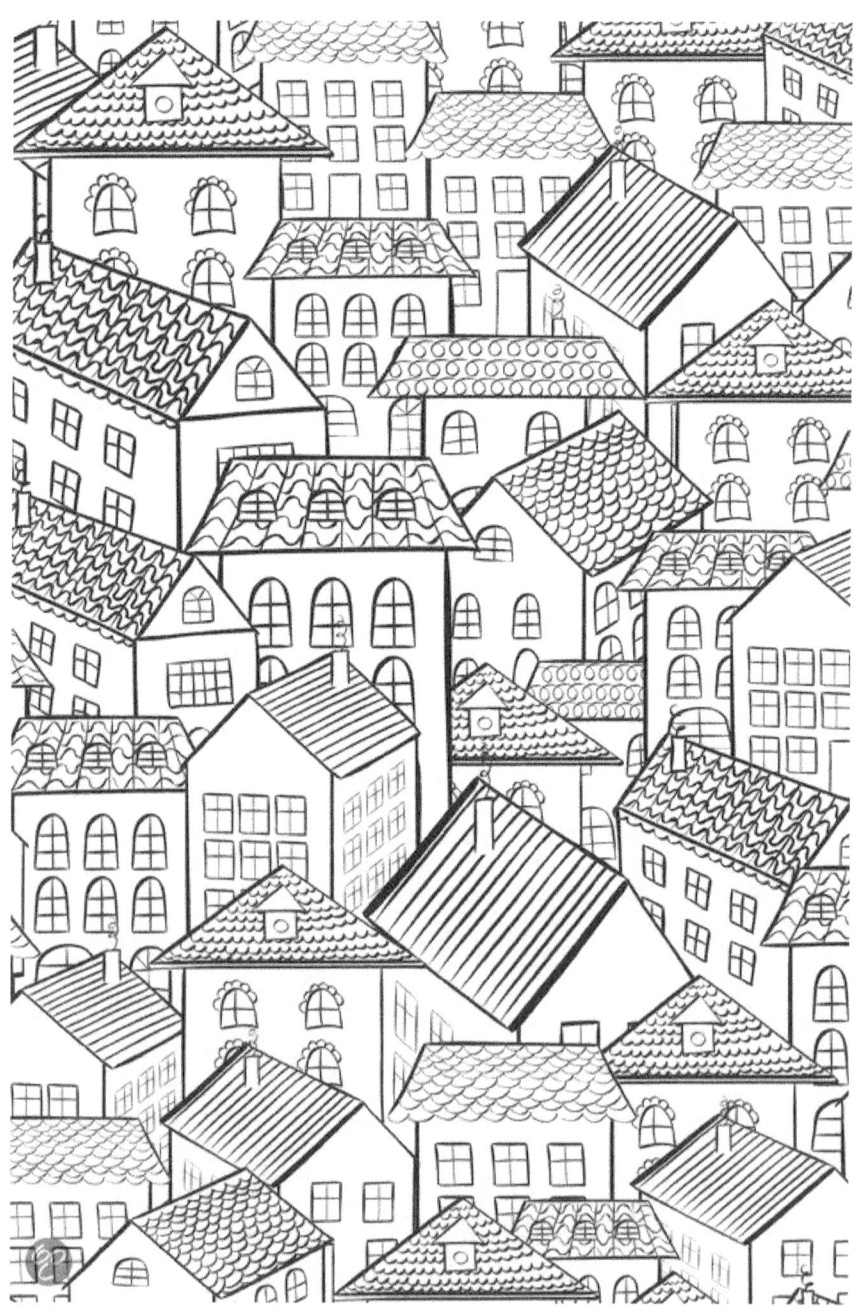

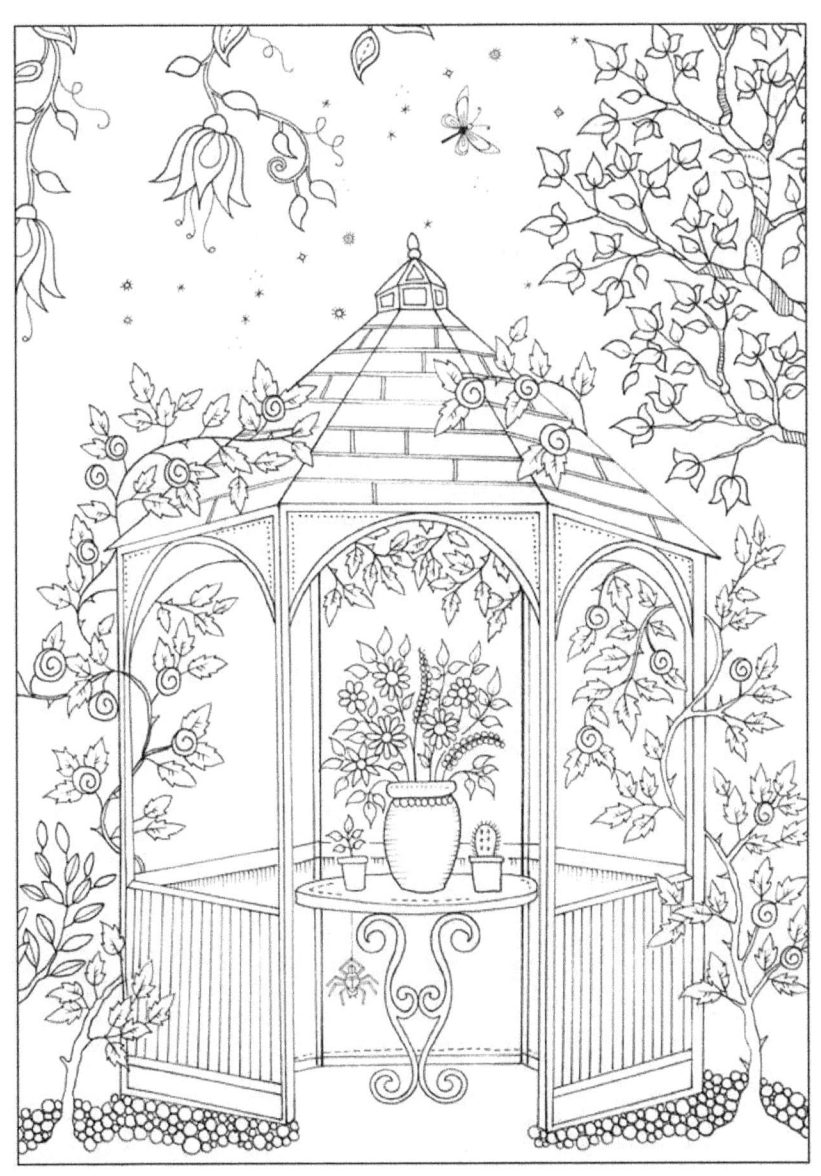

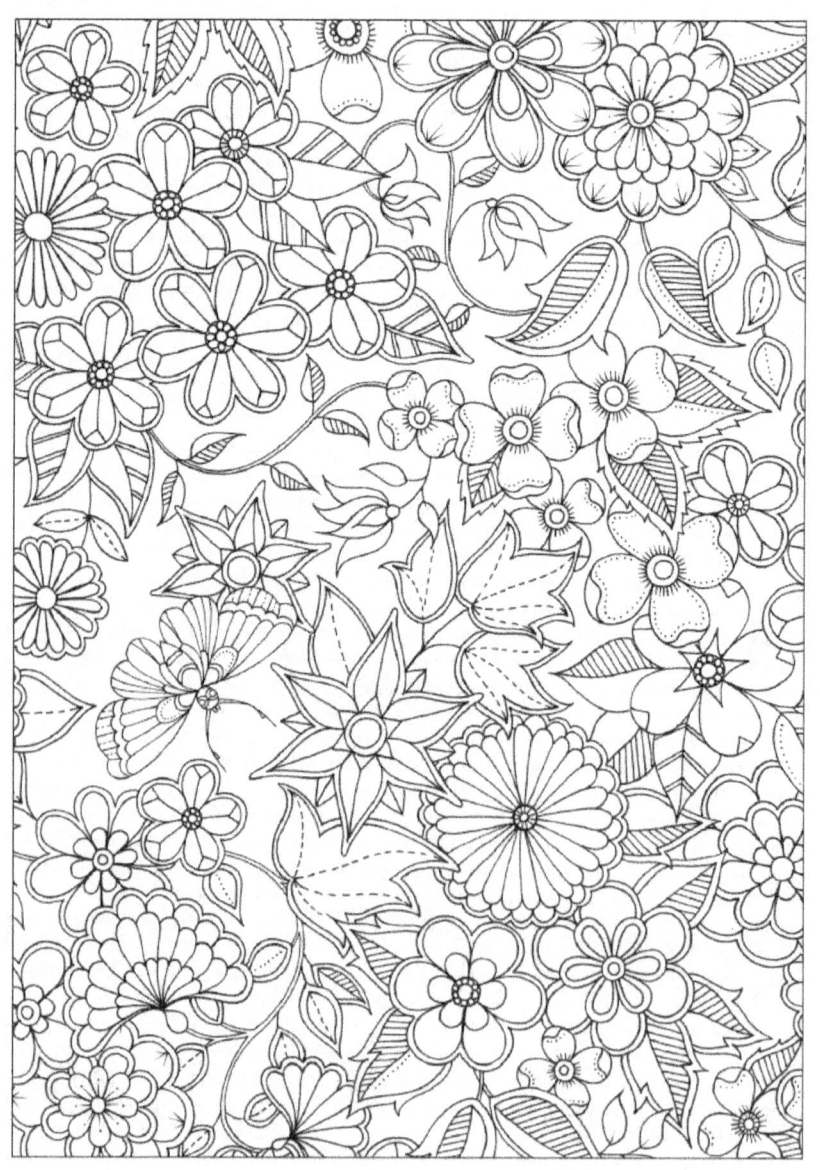

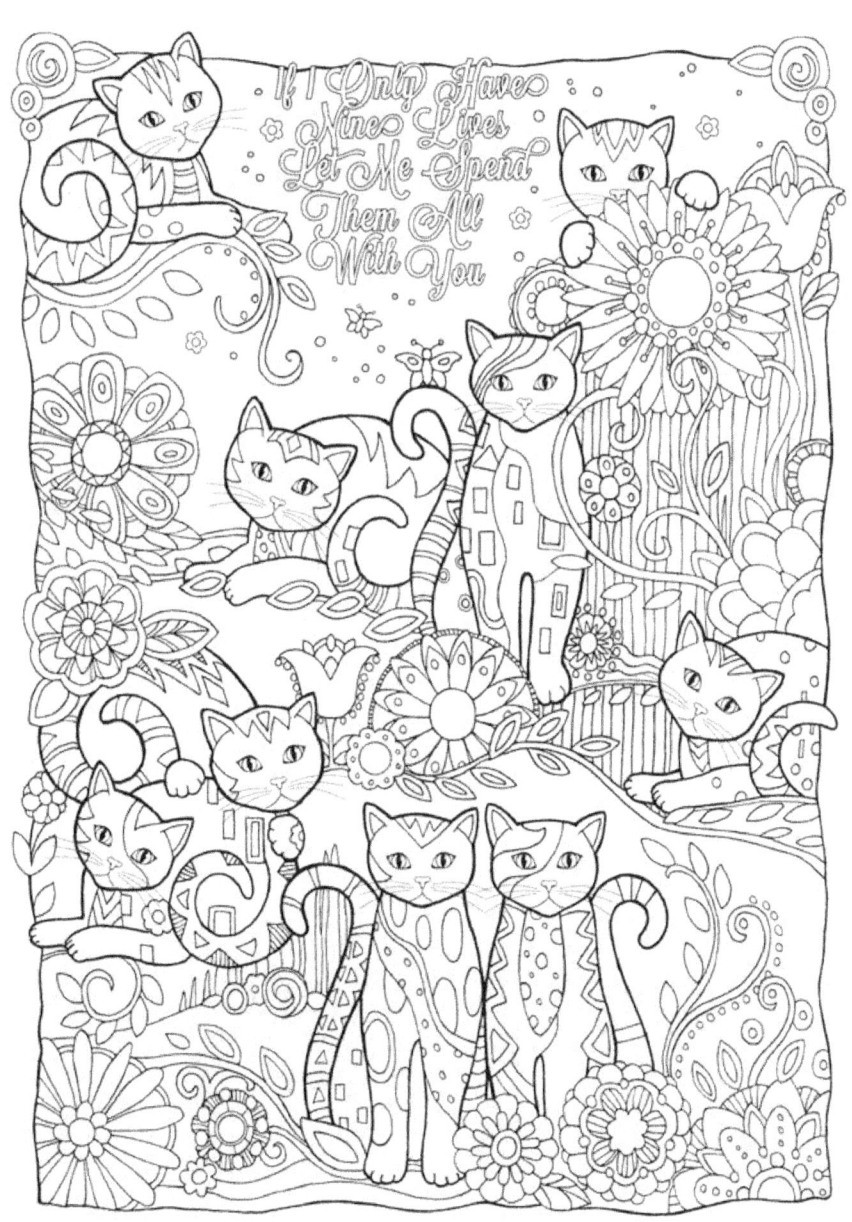

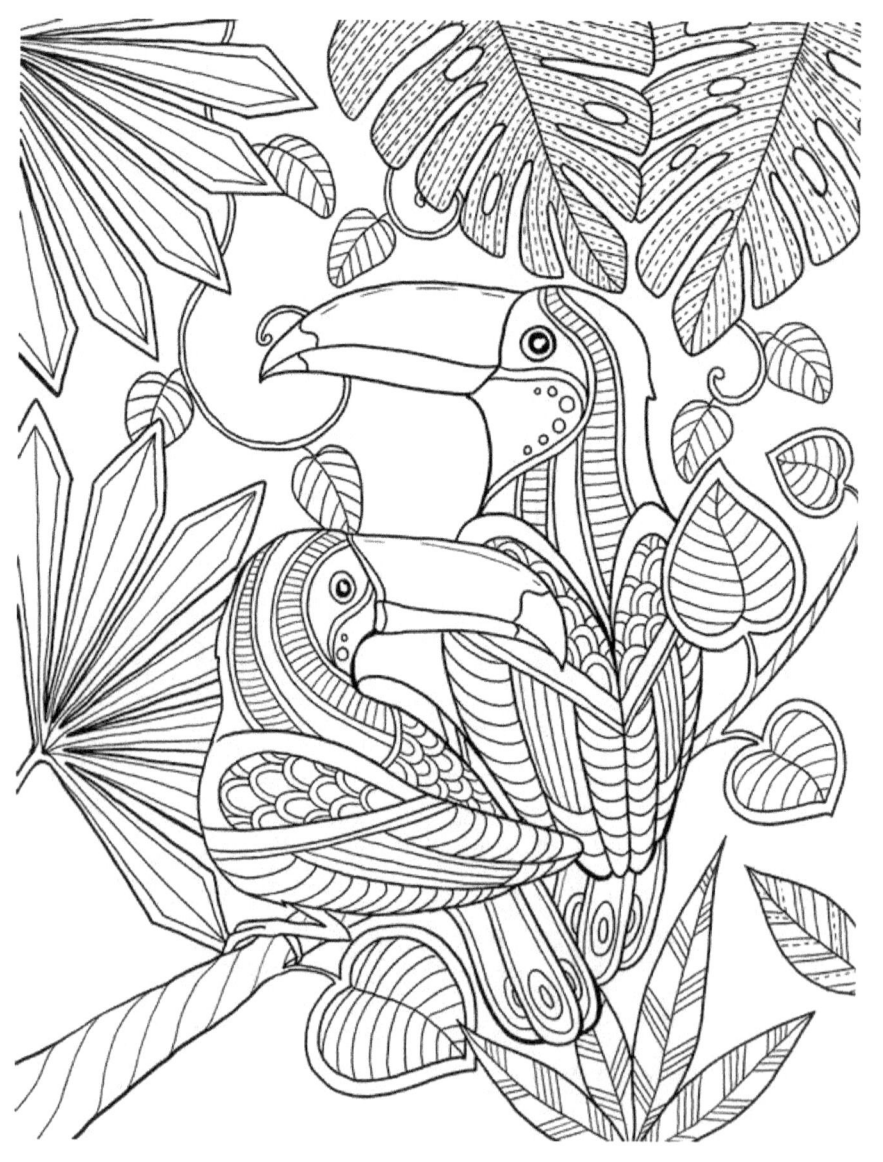

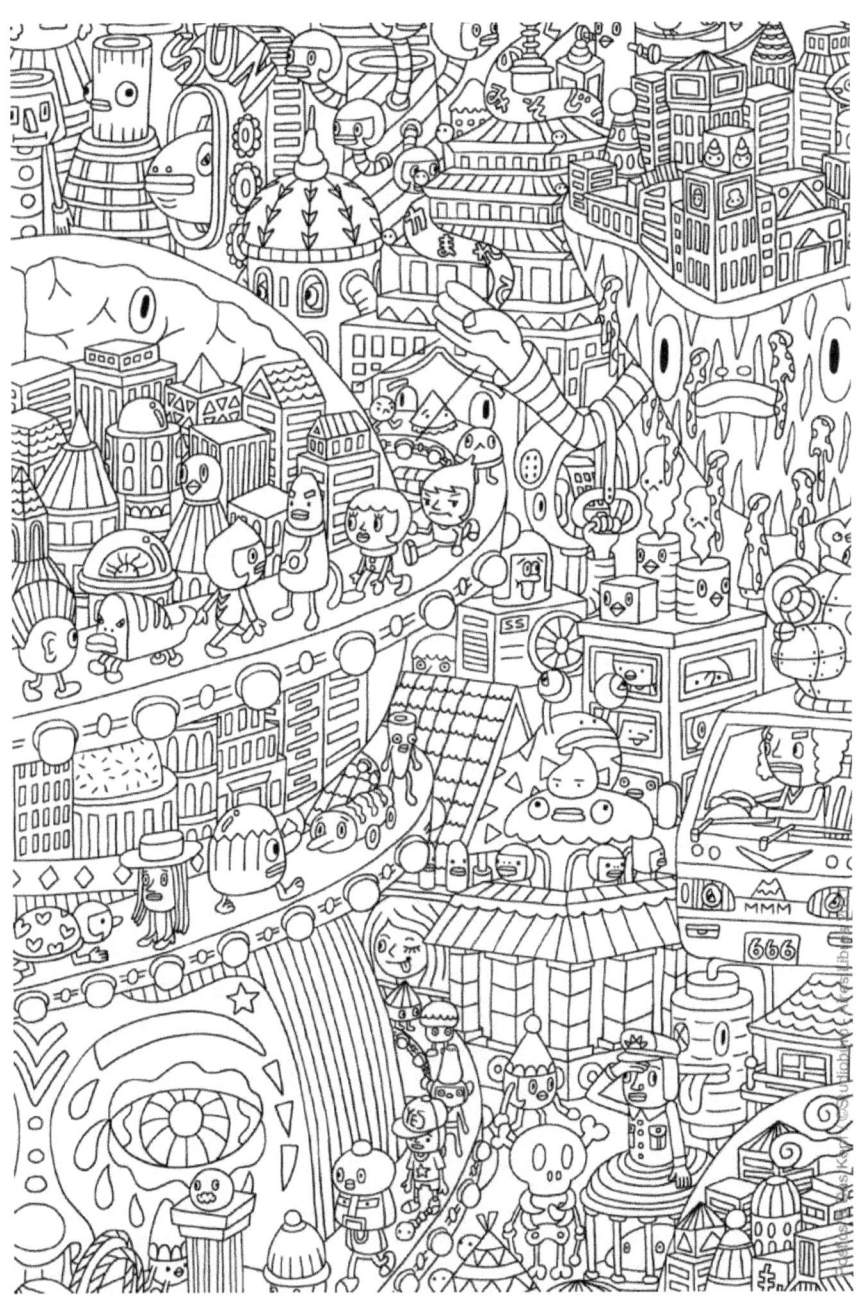

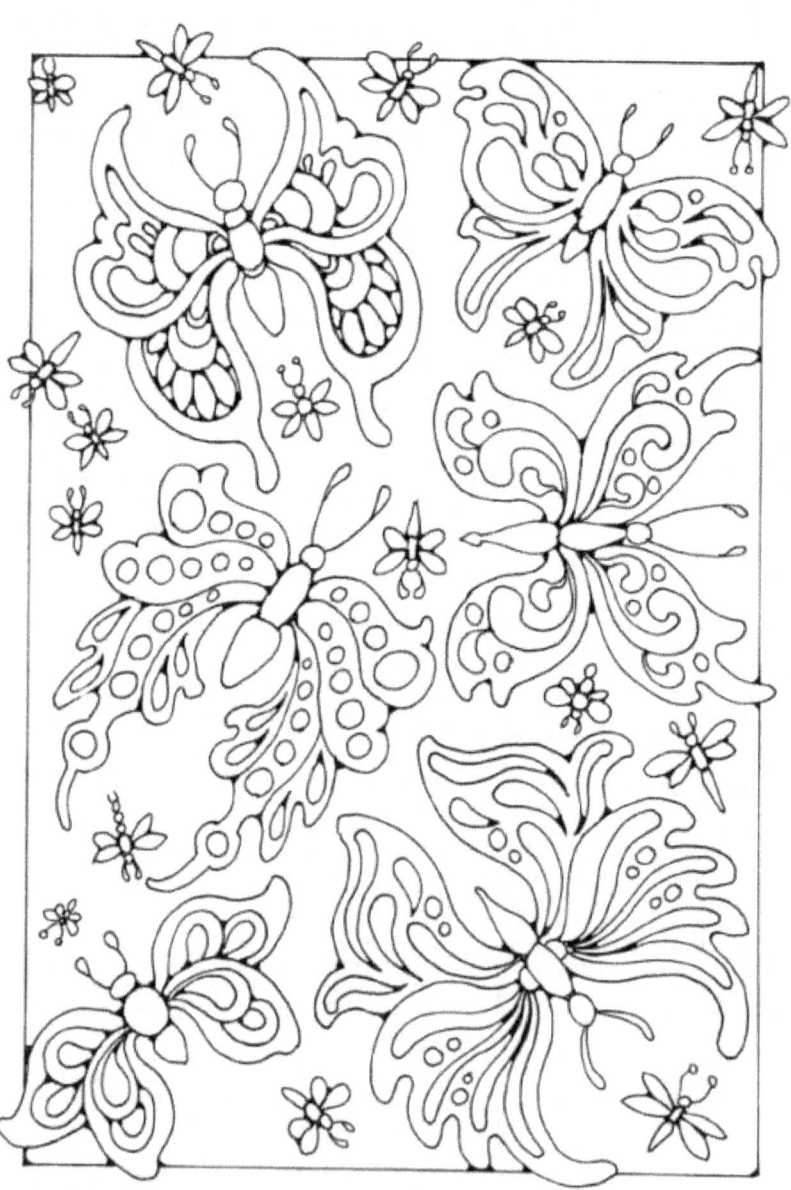

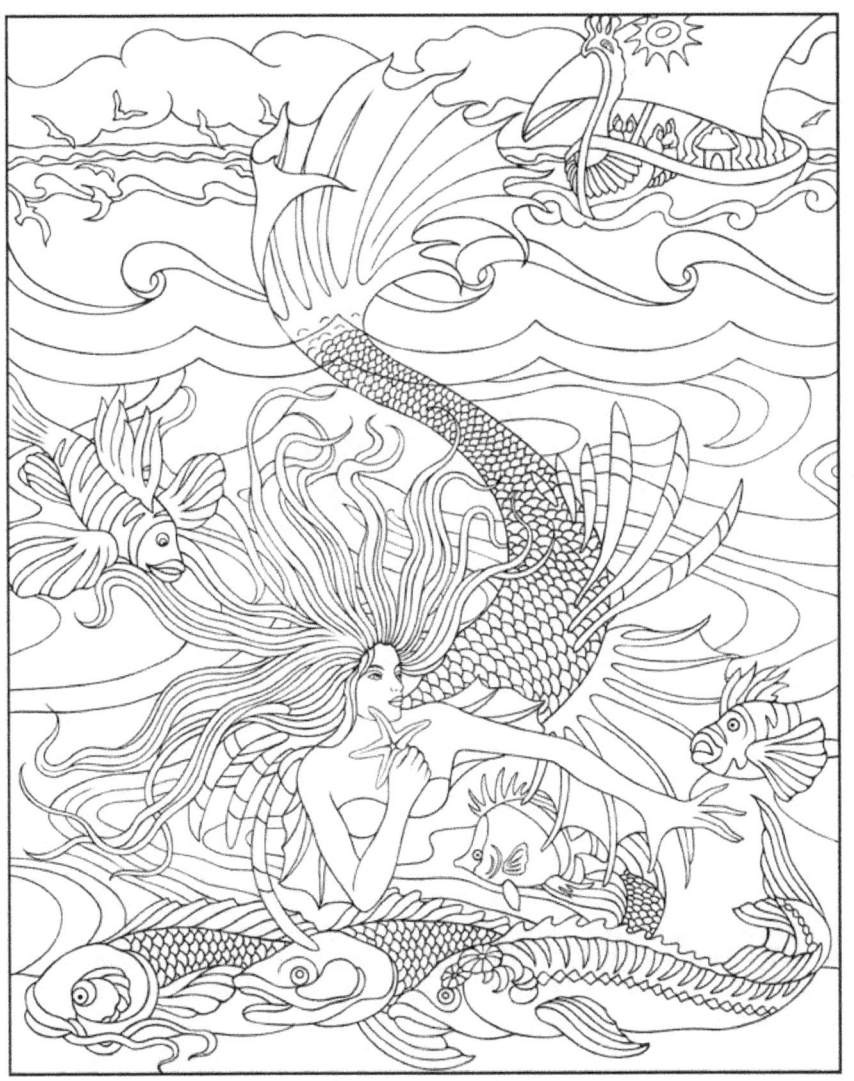

In this story from the United Kingdom, a young man with a beautiful voice enchanted the *Mermaid of Zennor* with his songs. He then left the land to live with her under the waters.

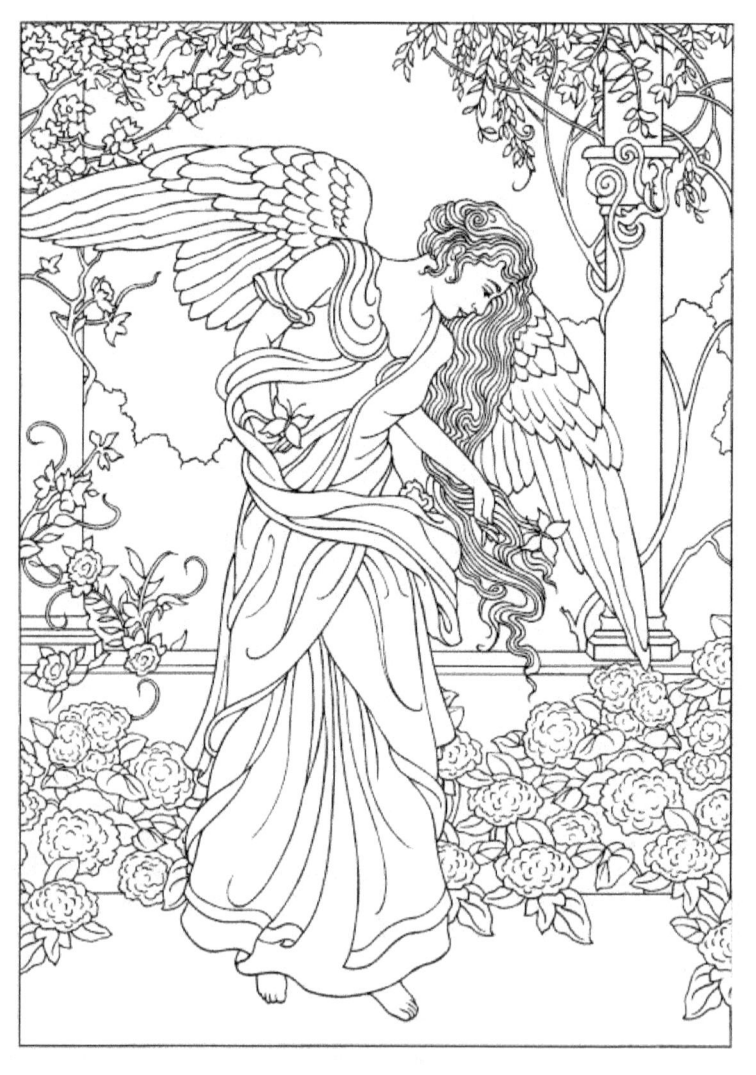

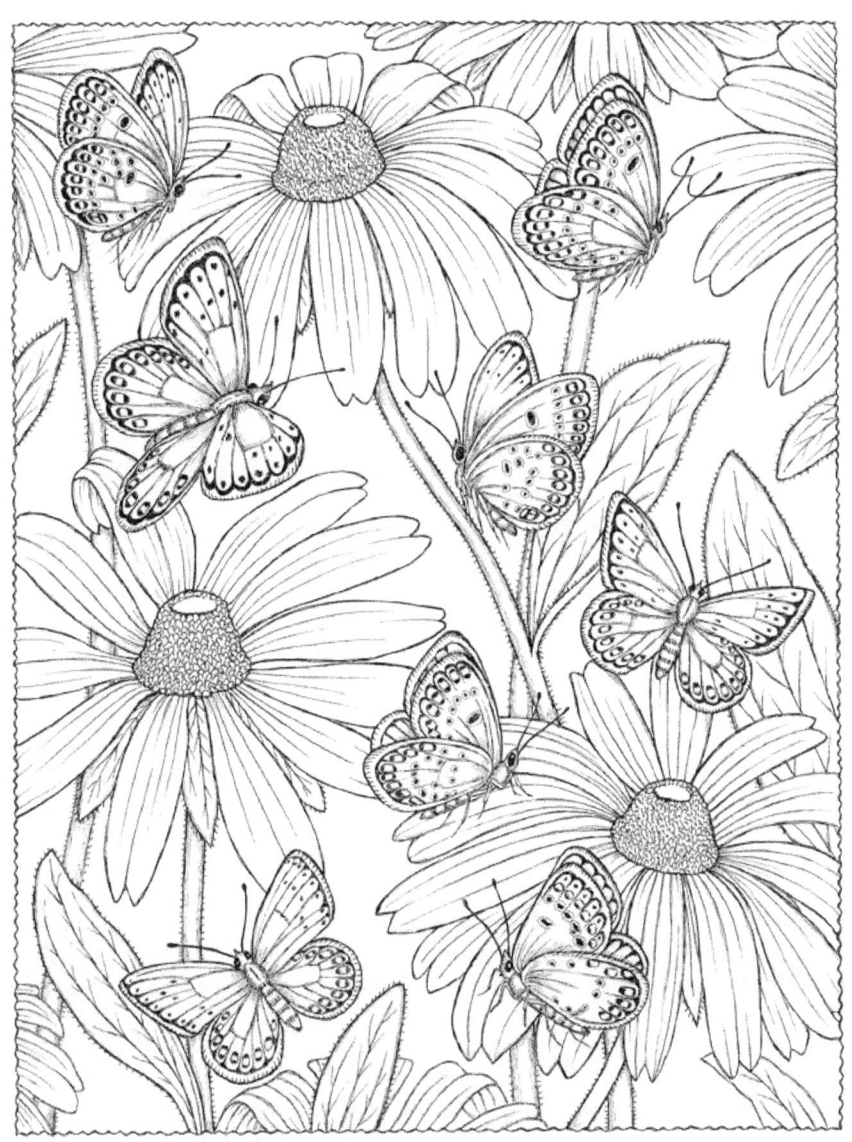

Blue butterflies and black-eyed Susans

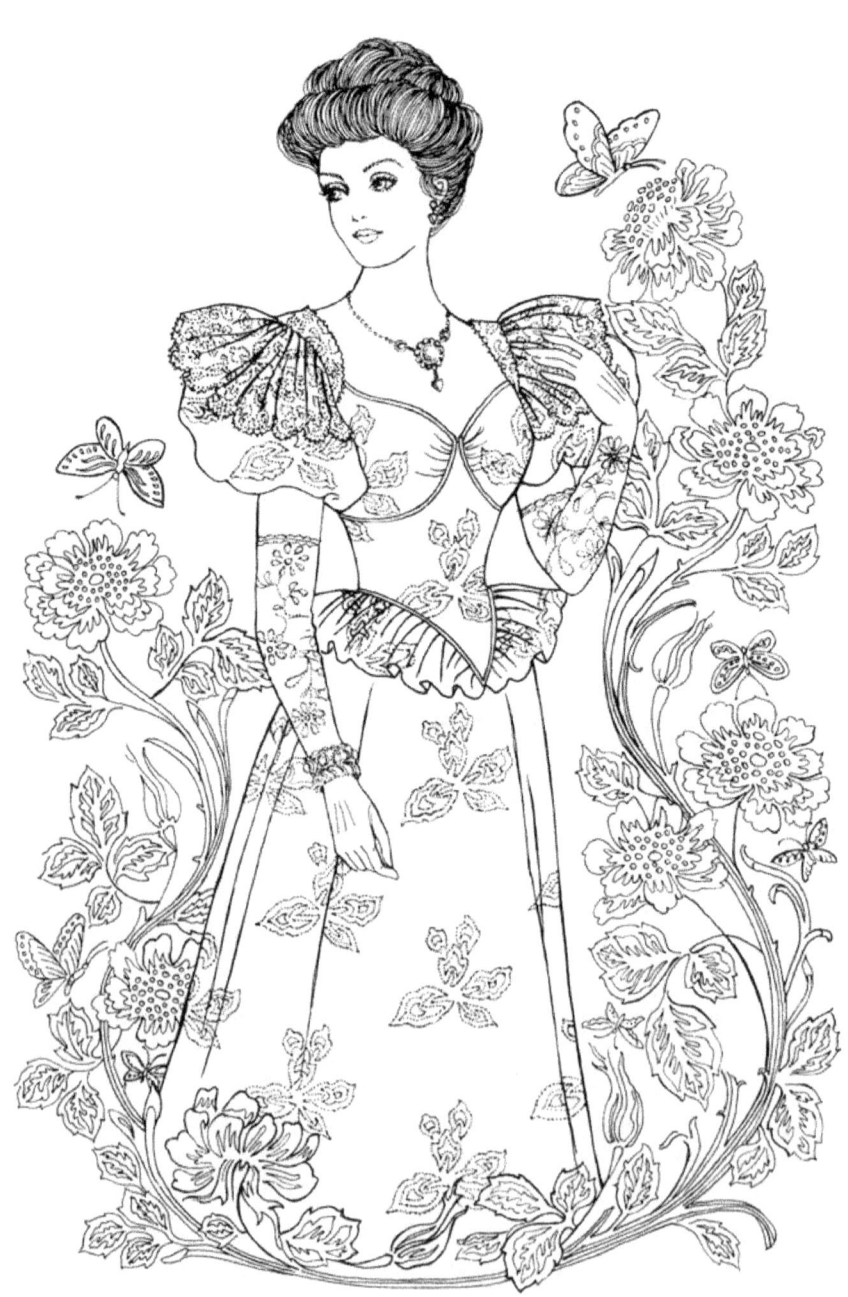

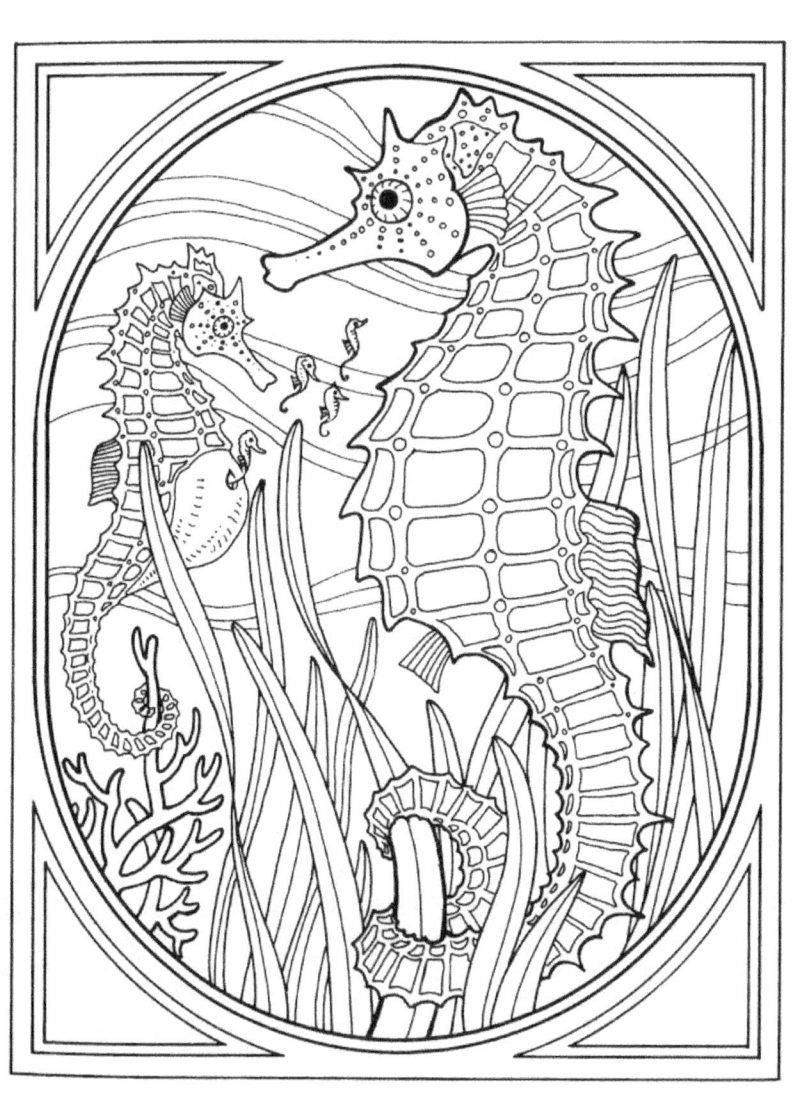

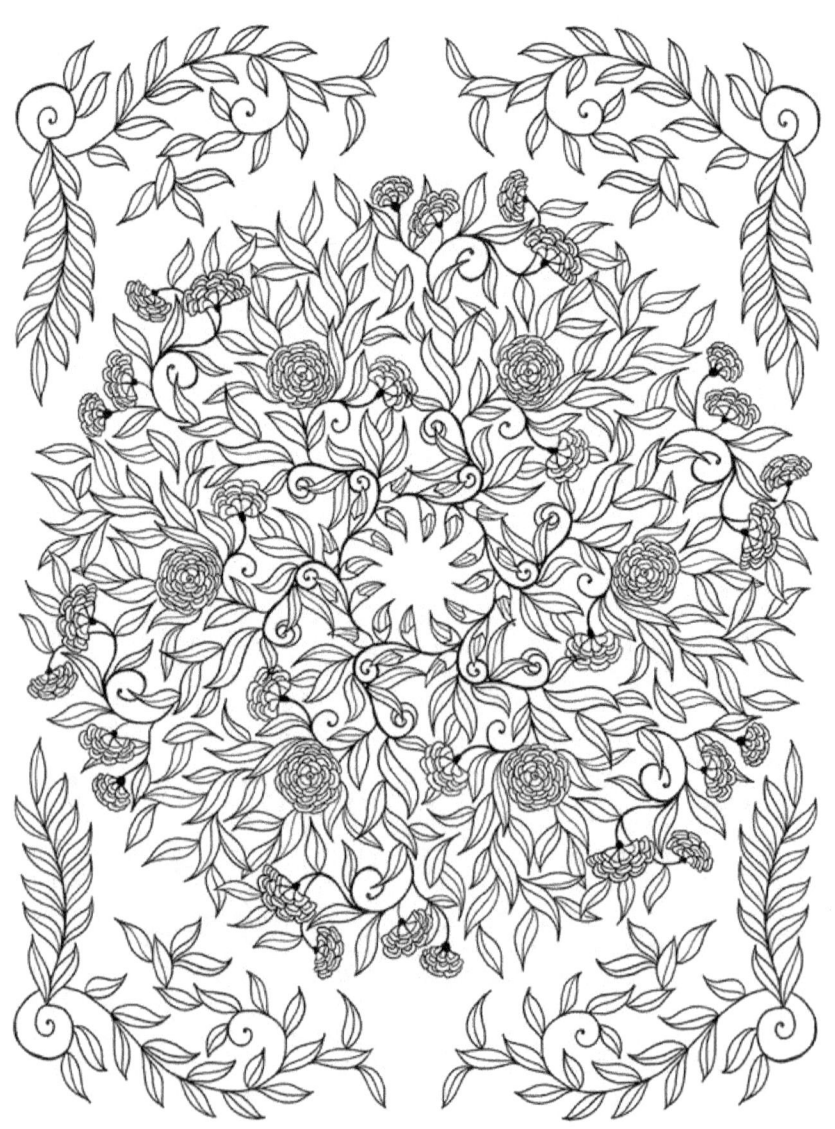

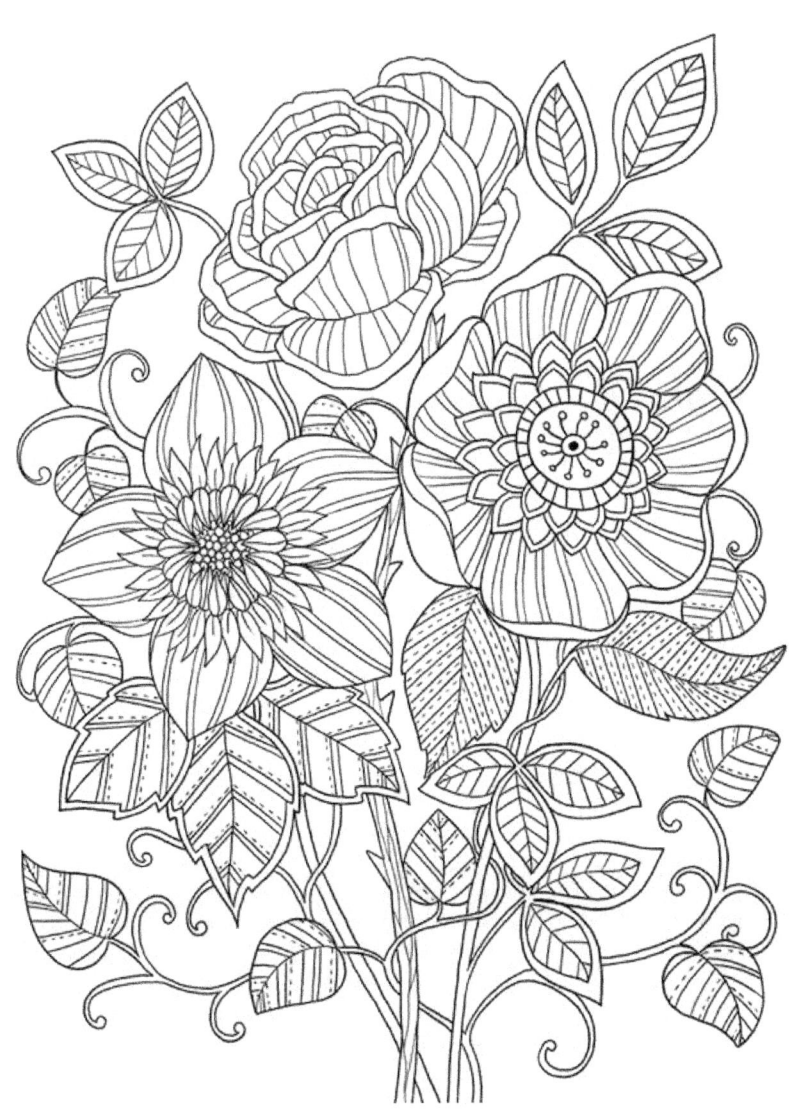

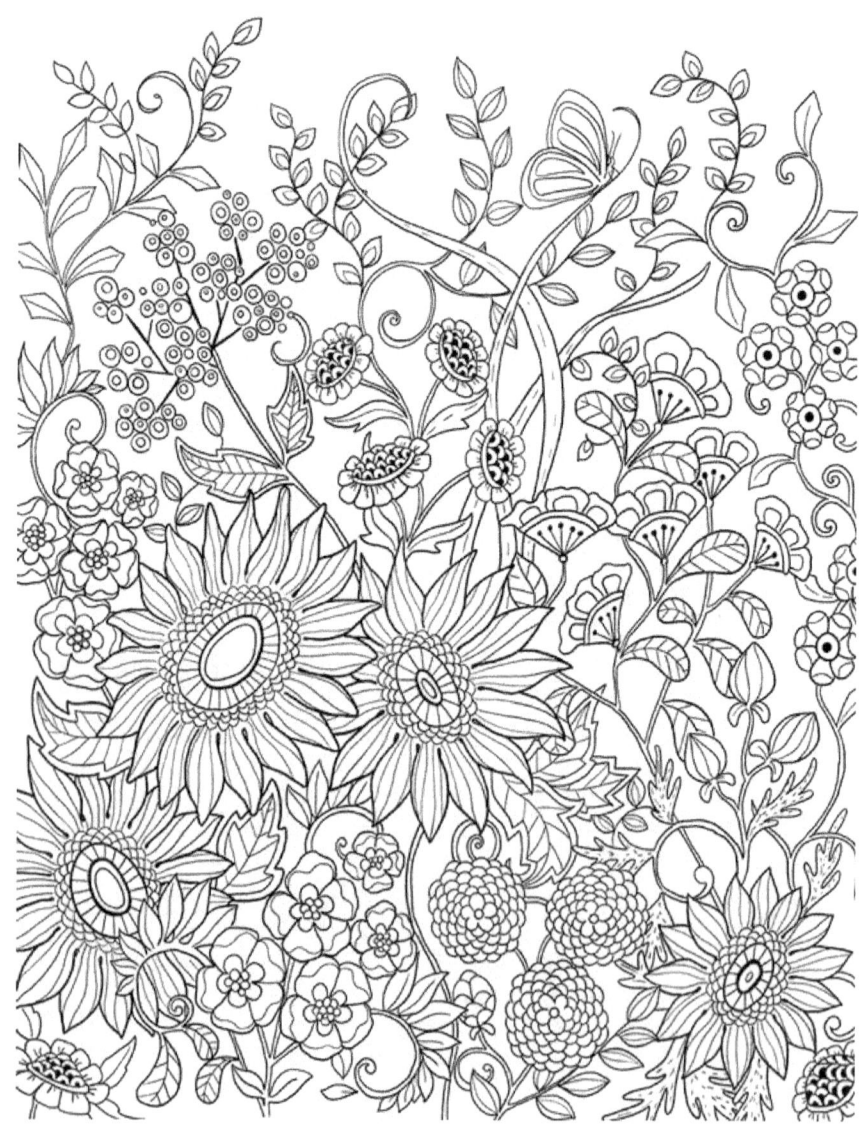

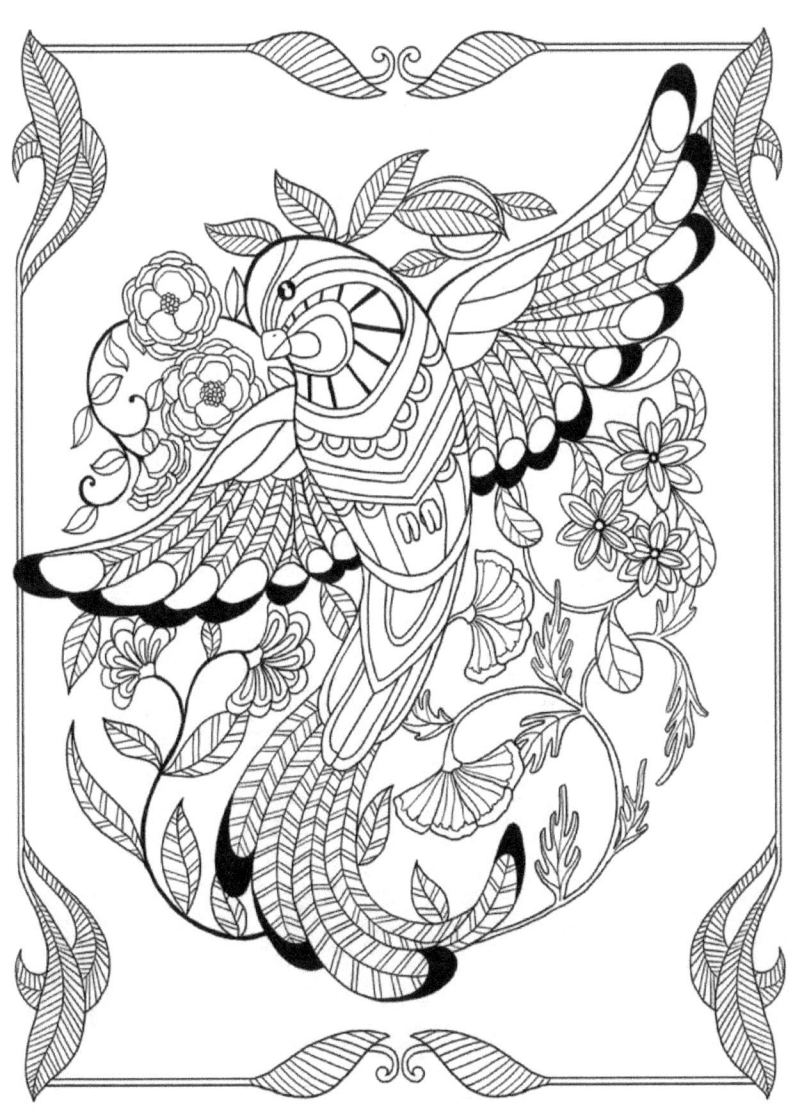

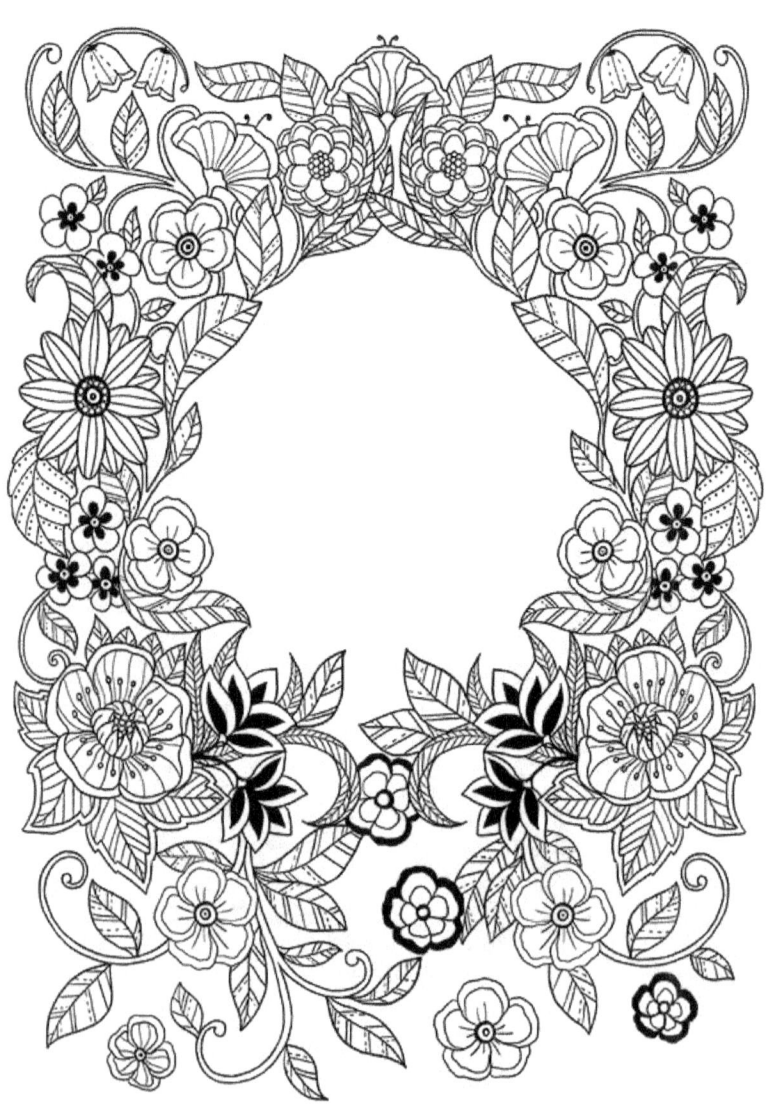

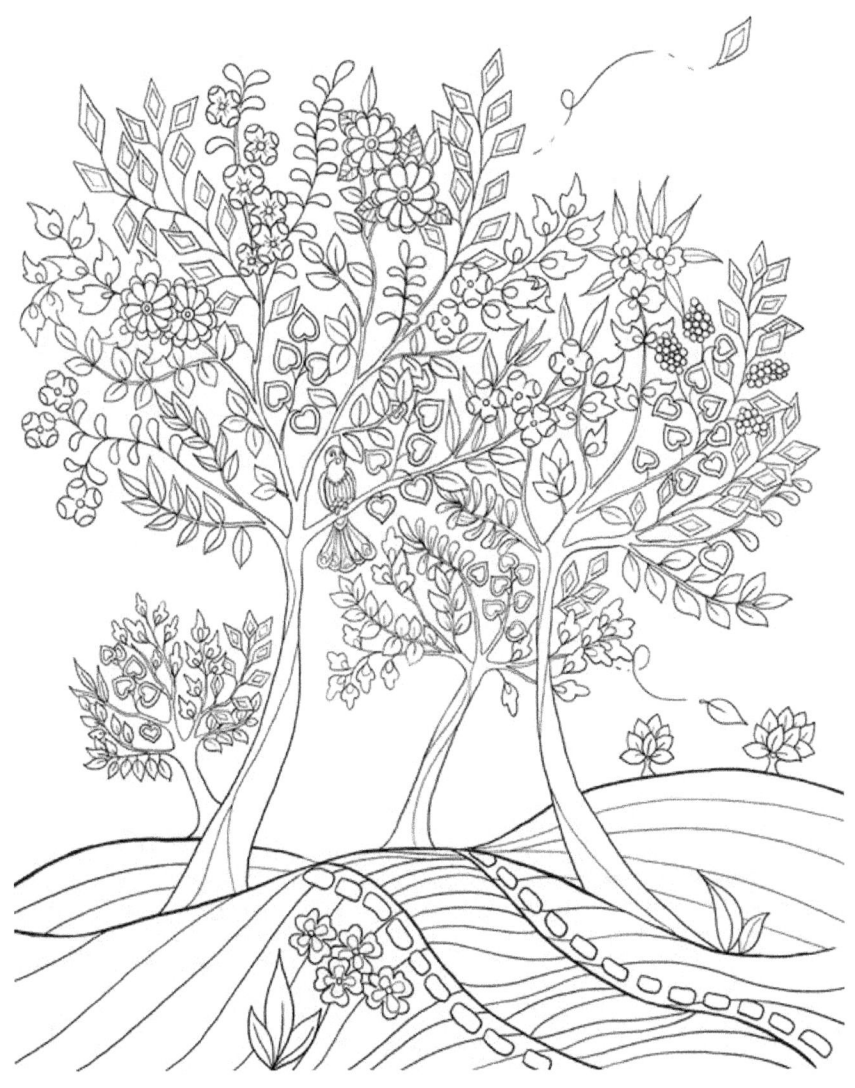

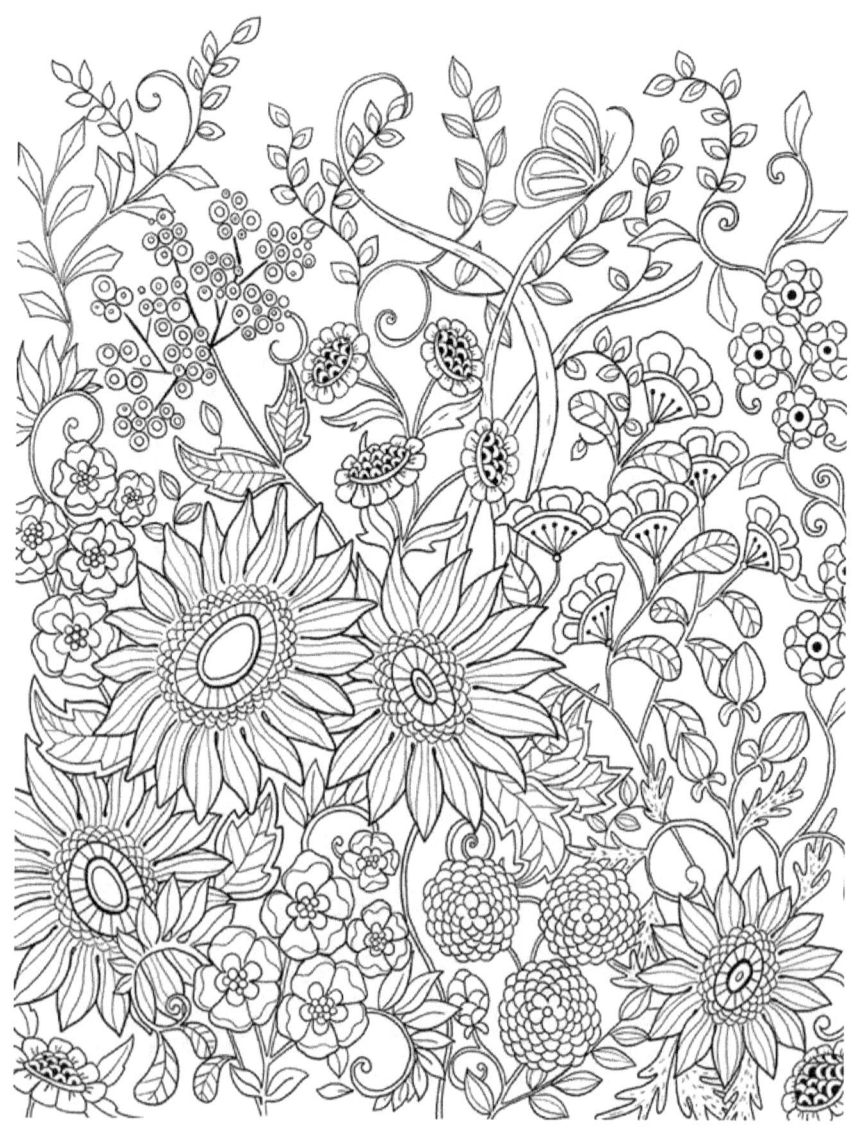

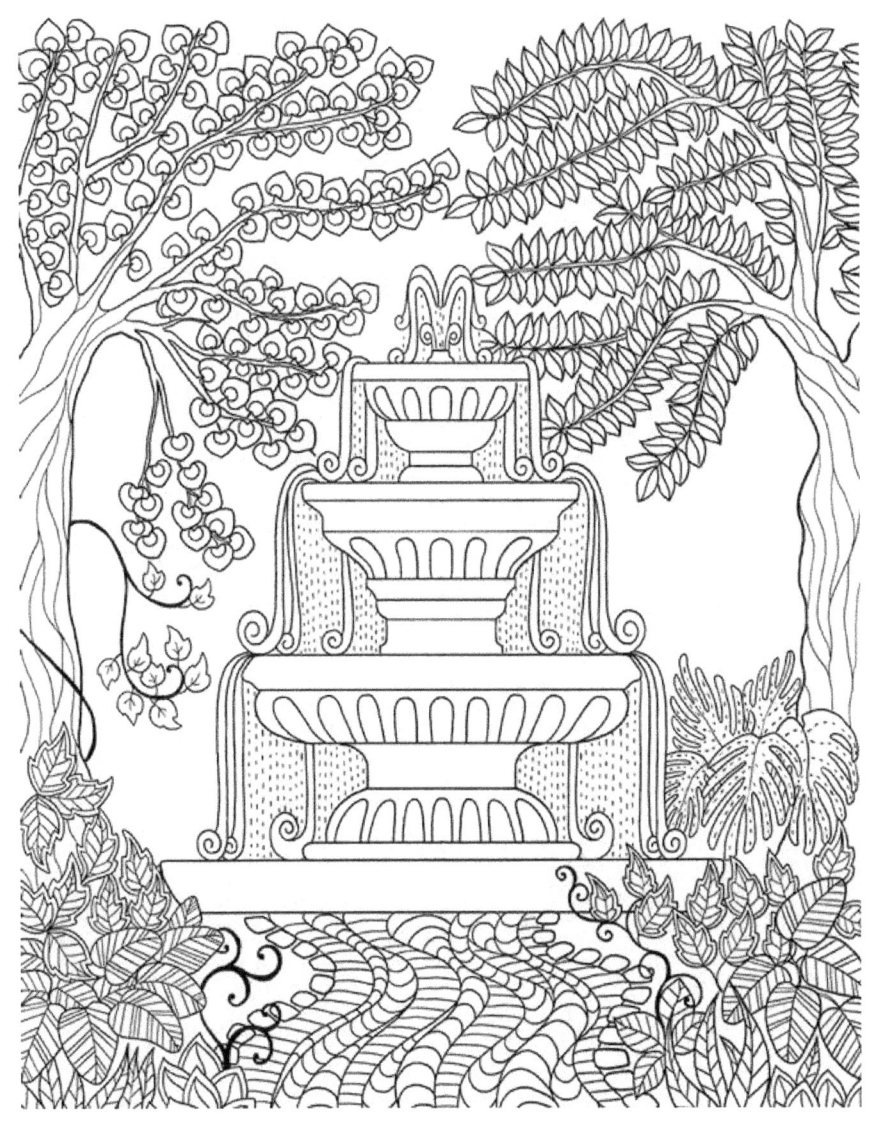

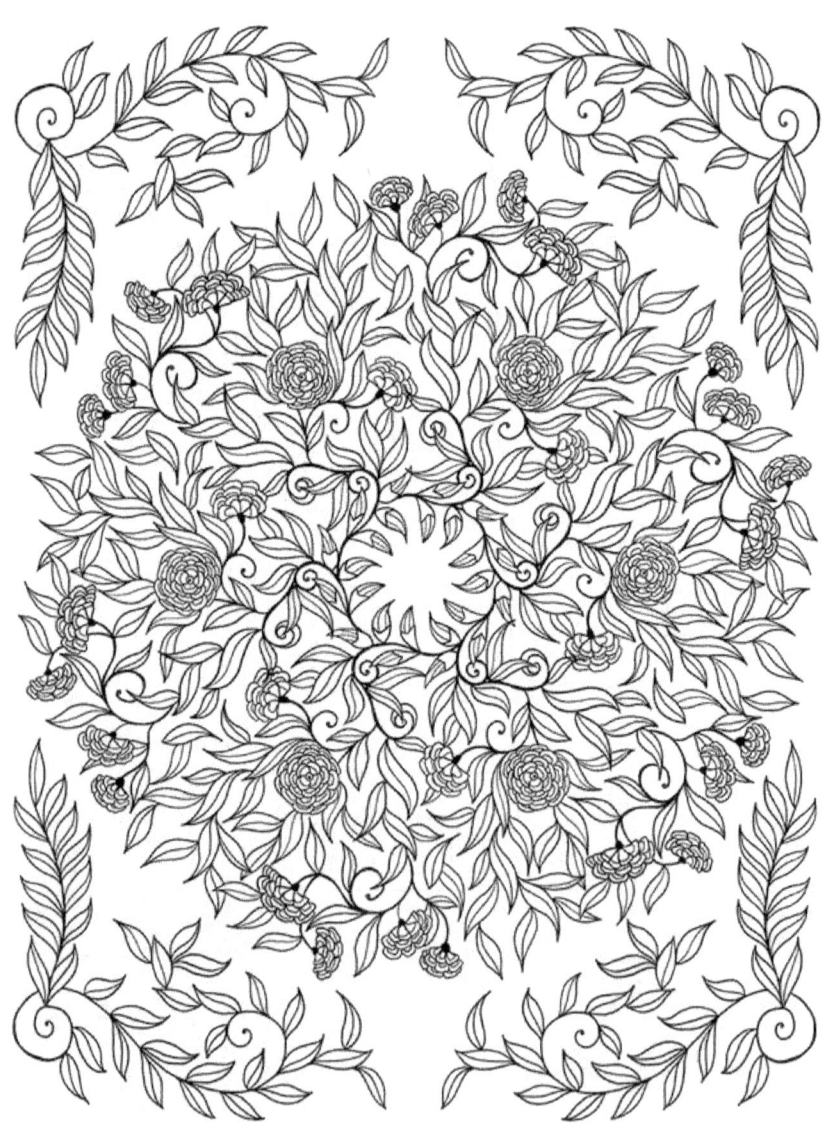

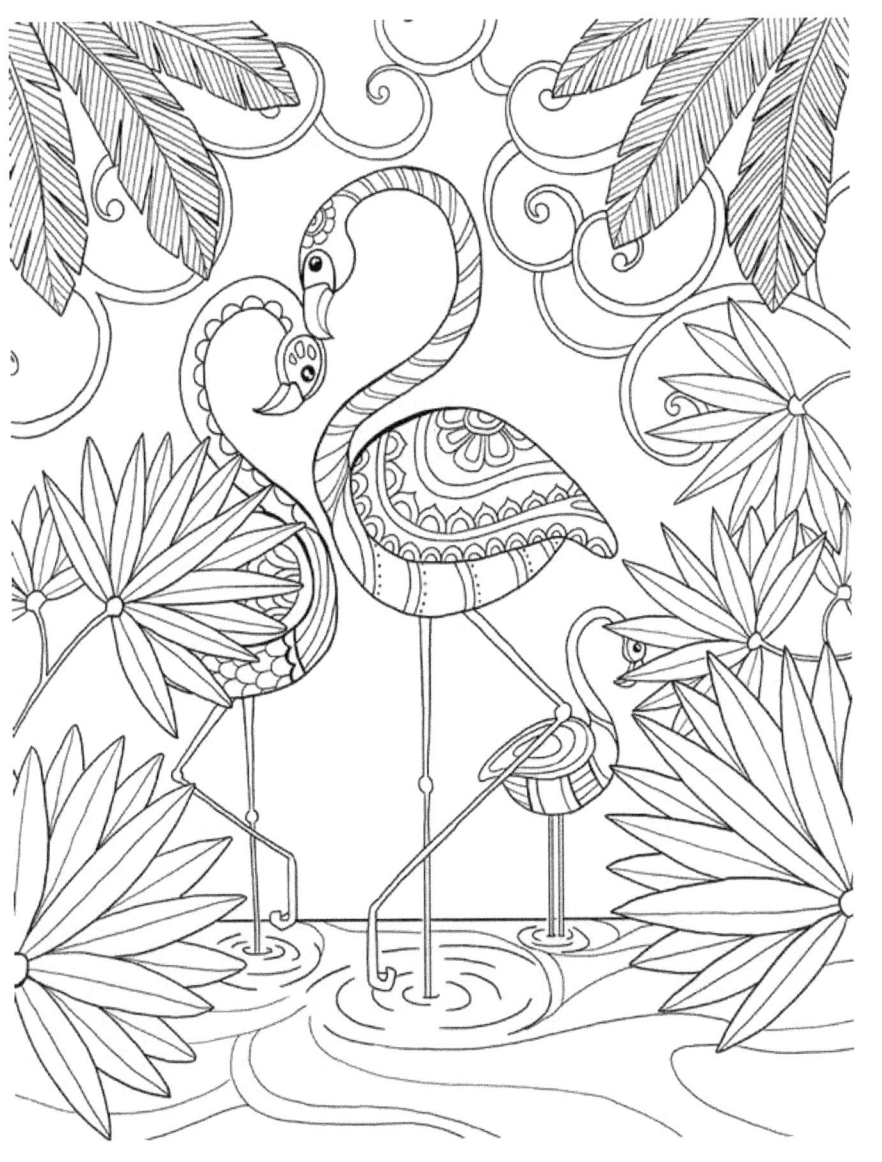

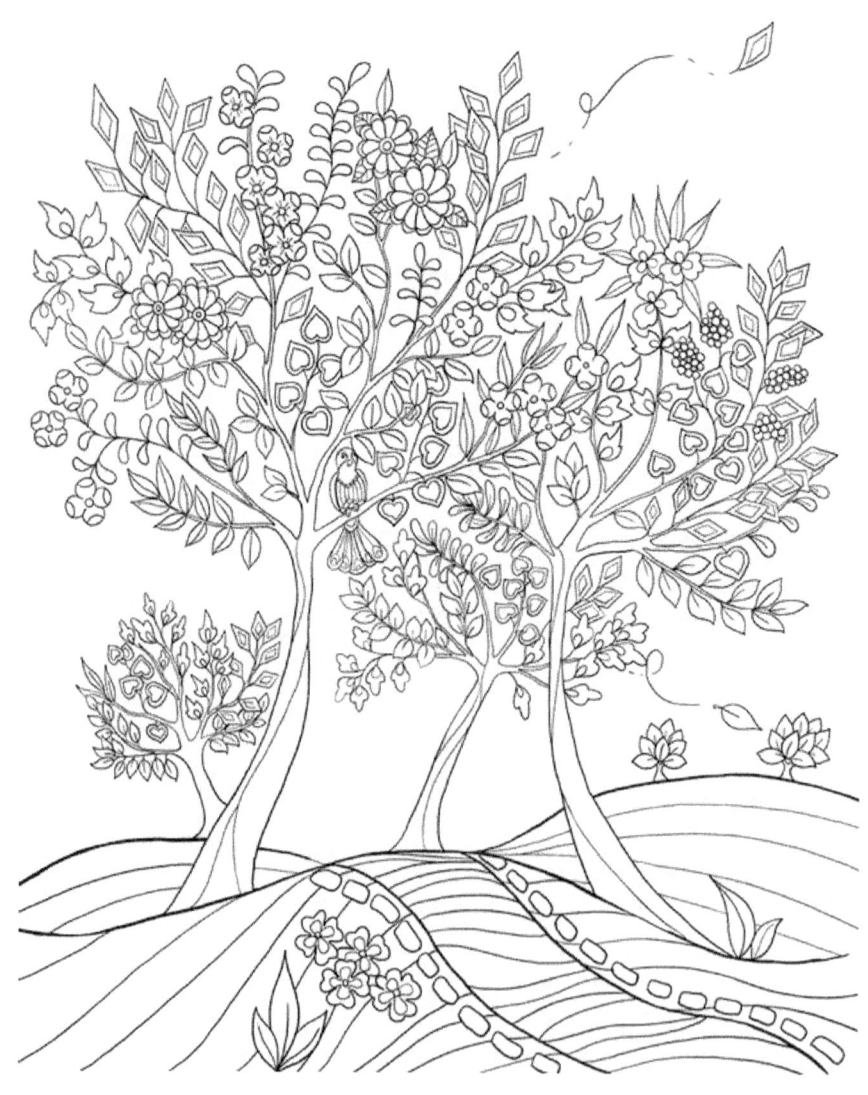

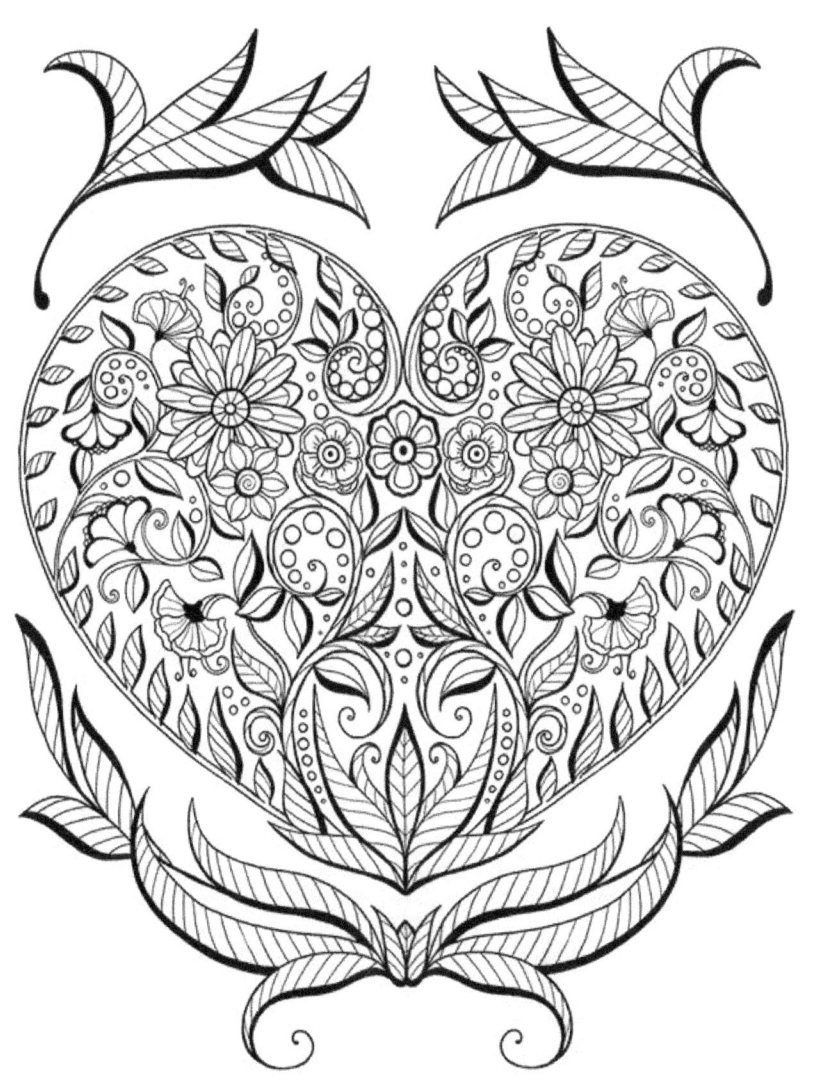

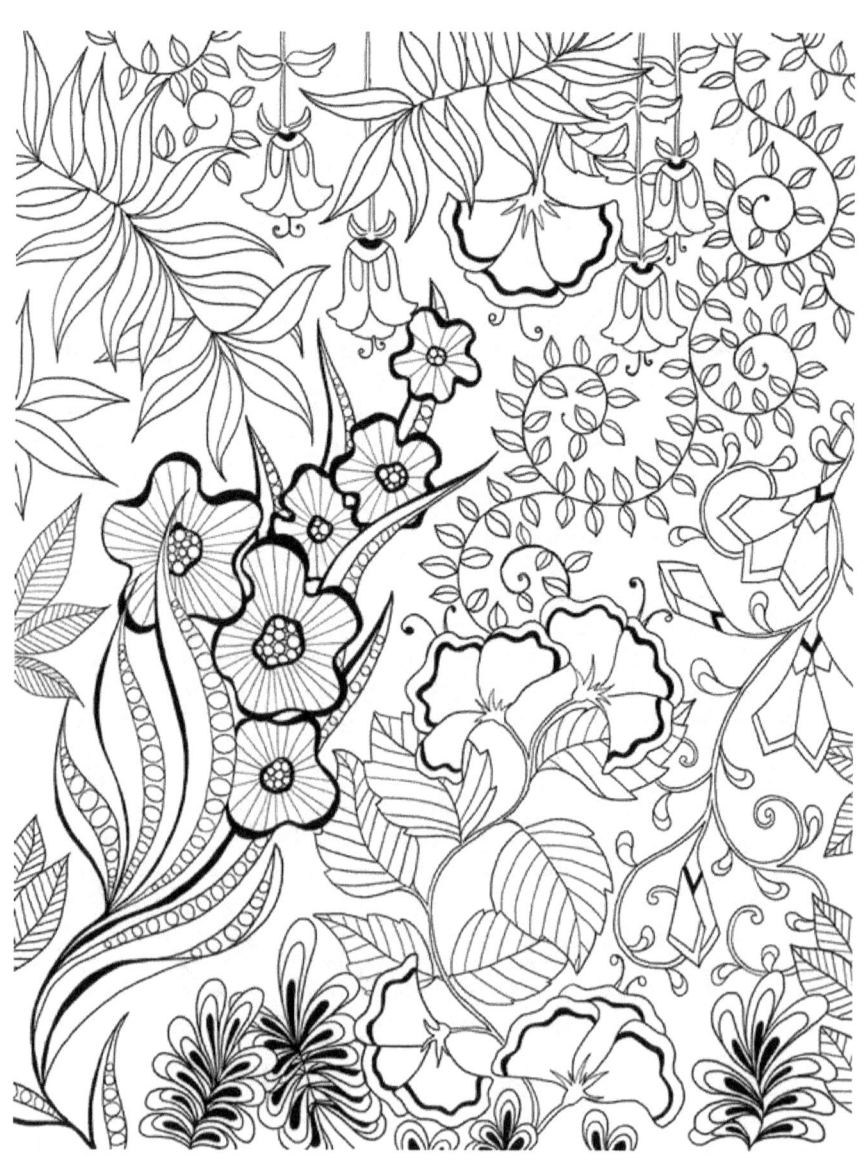

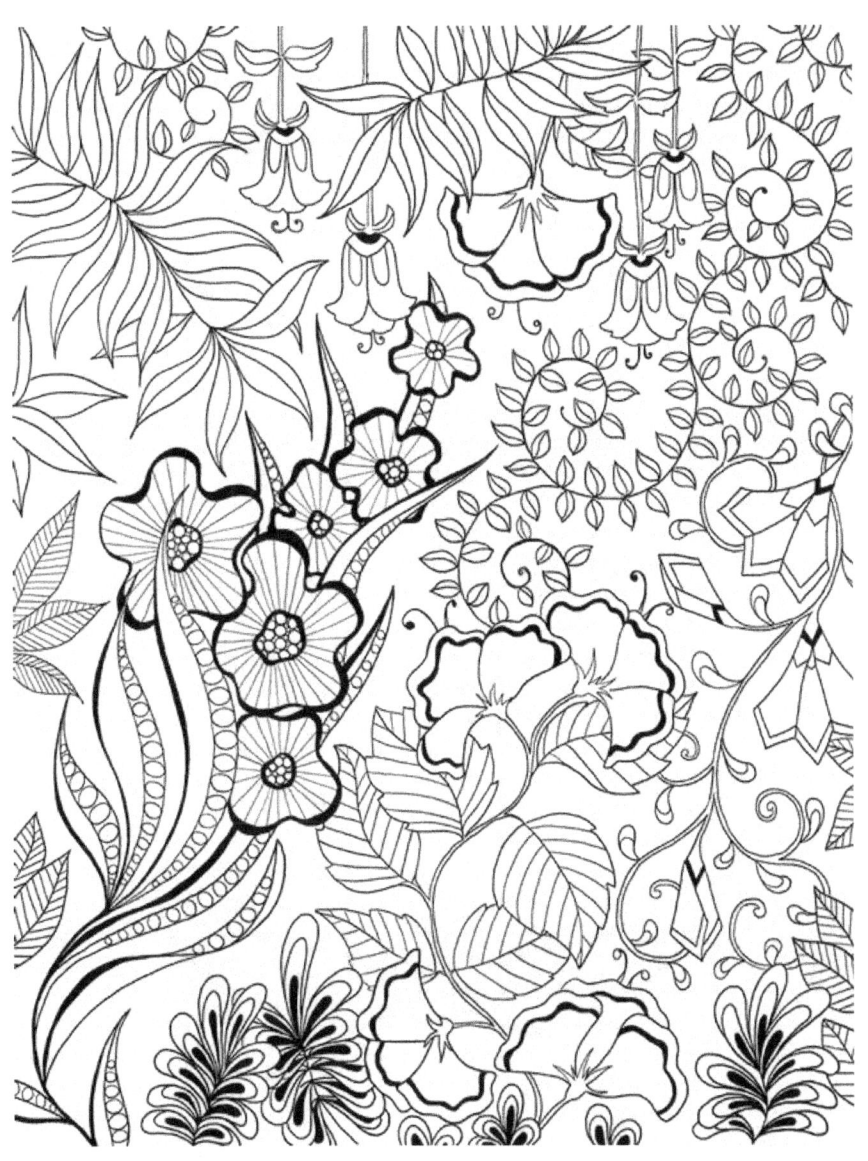

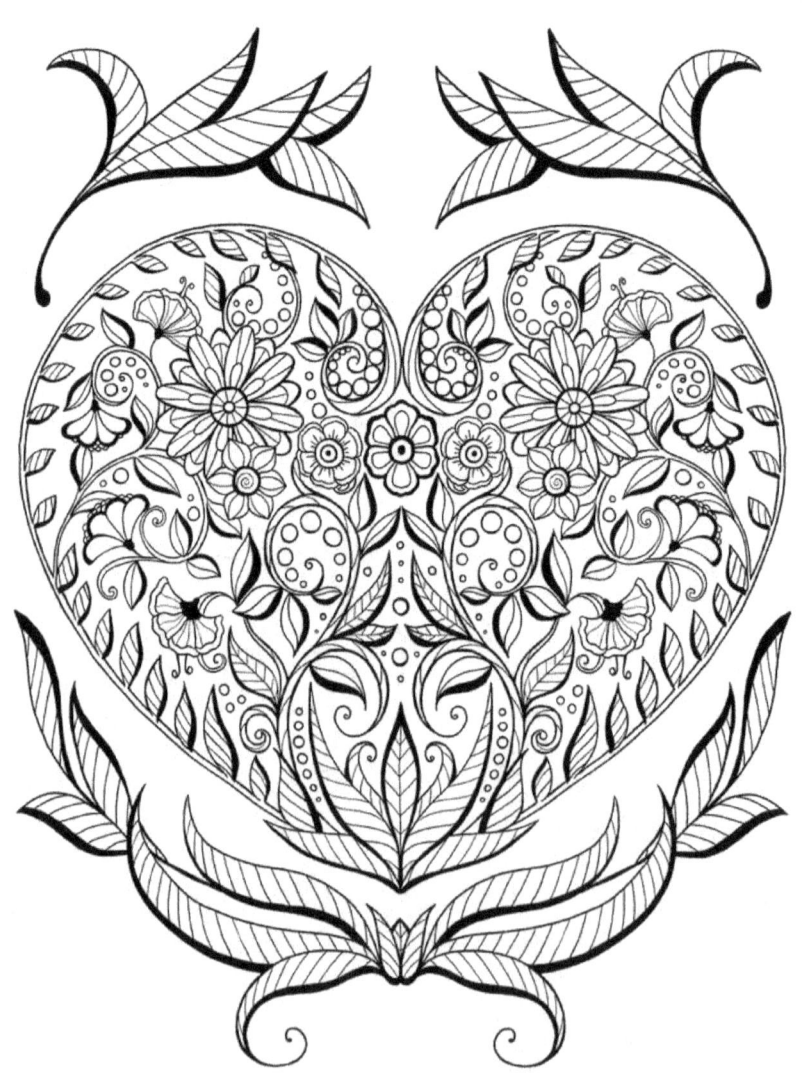

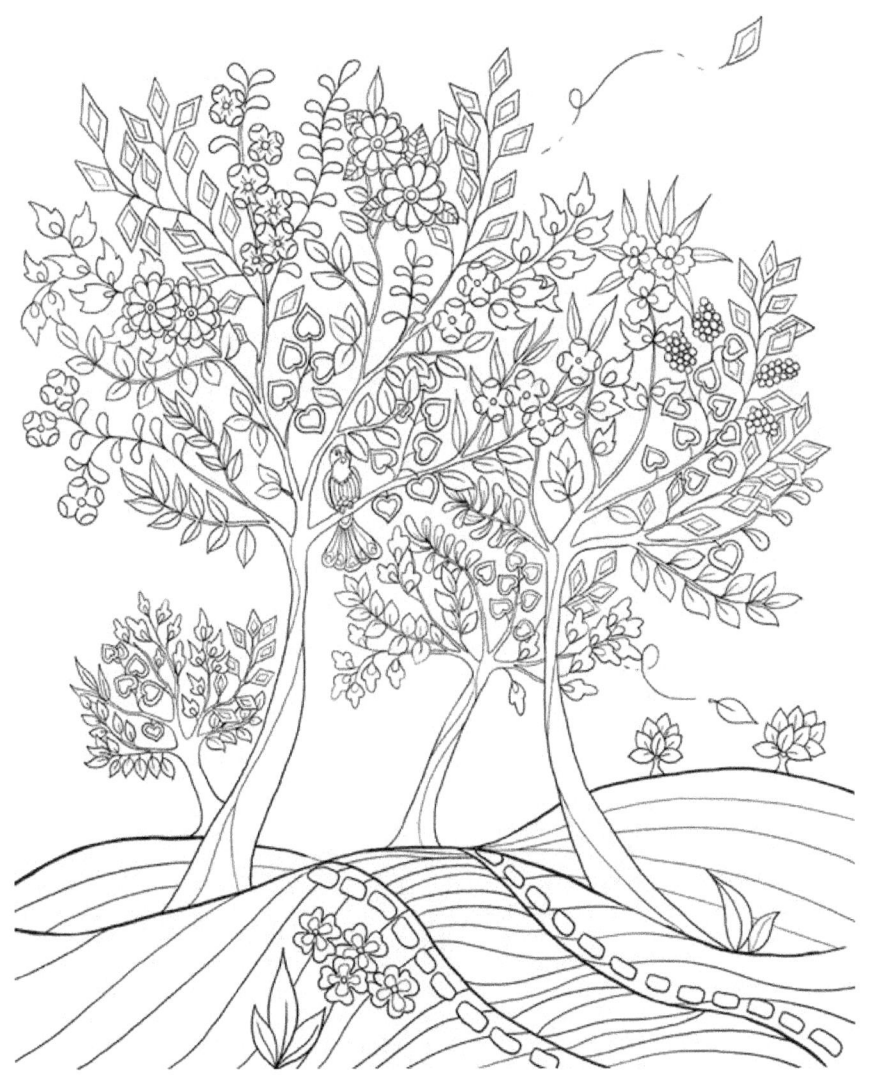

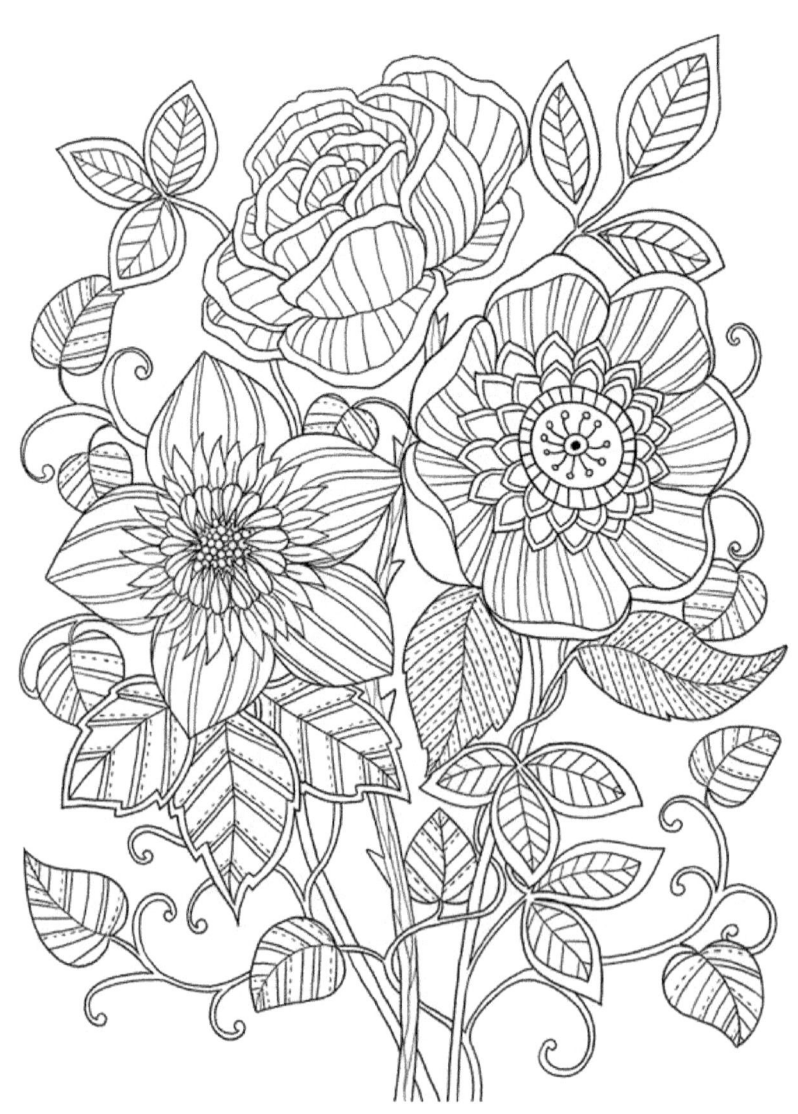

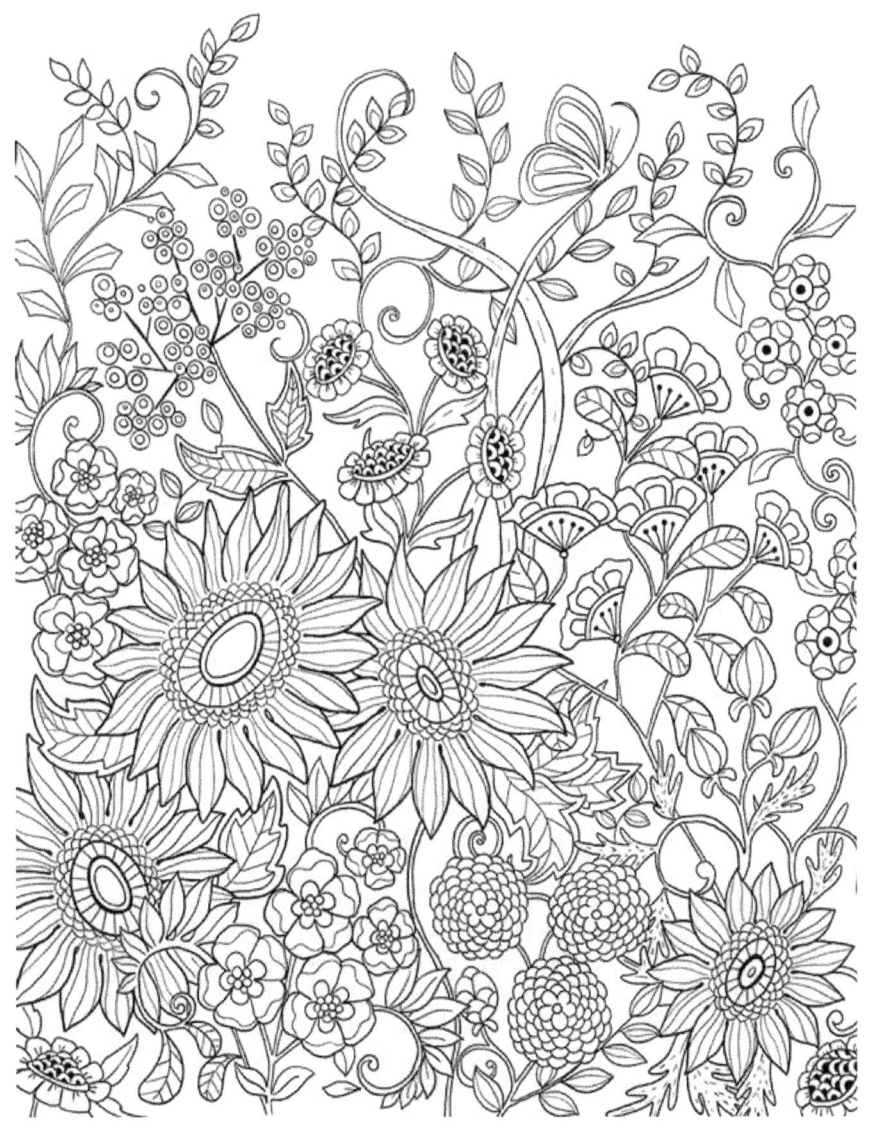

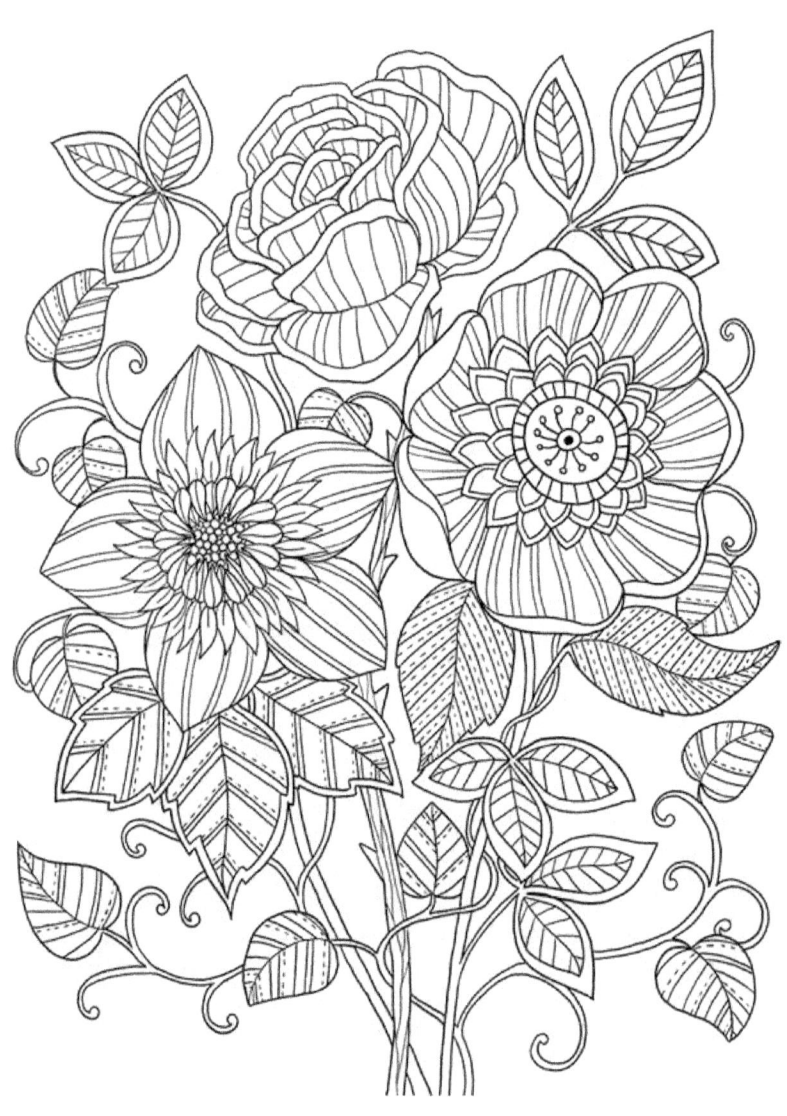

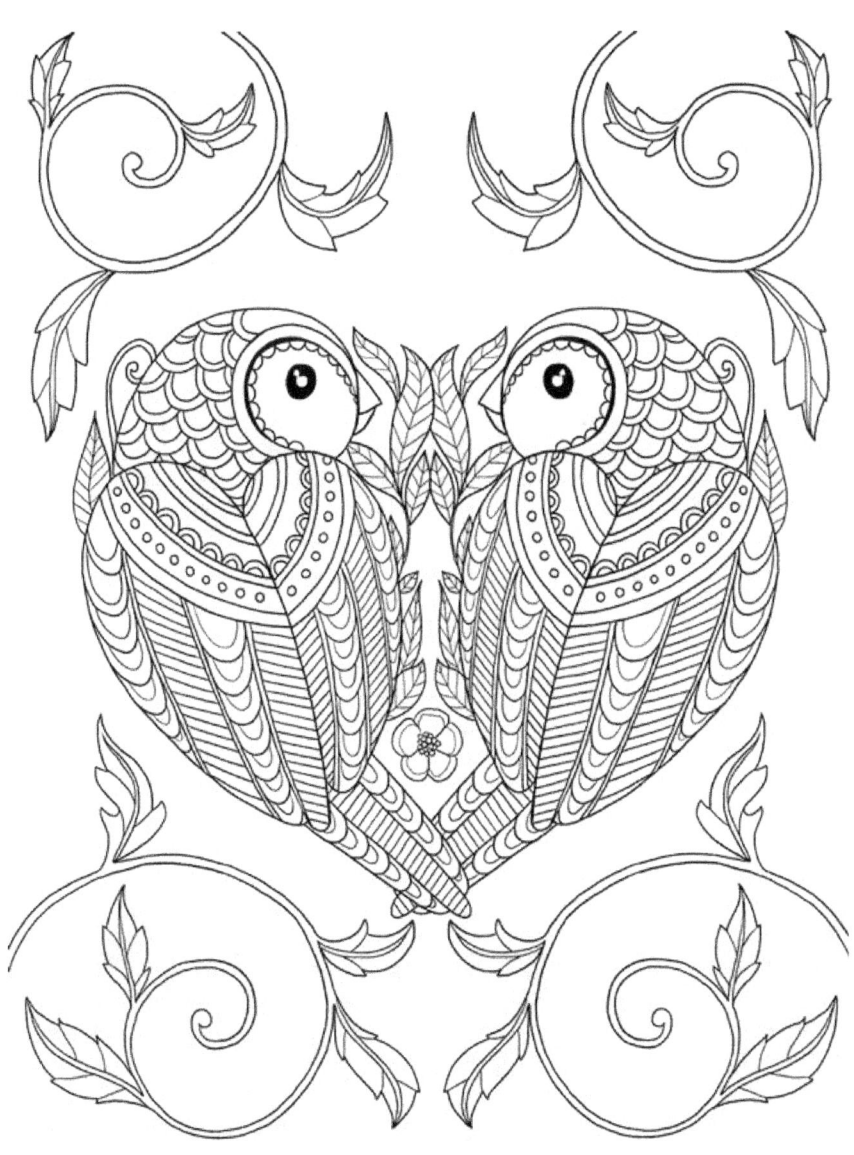

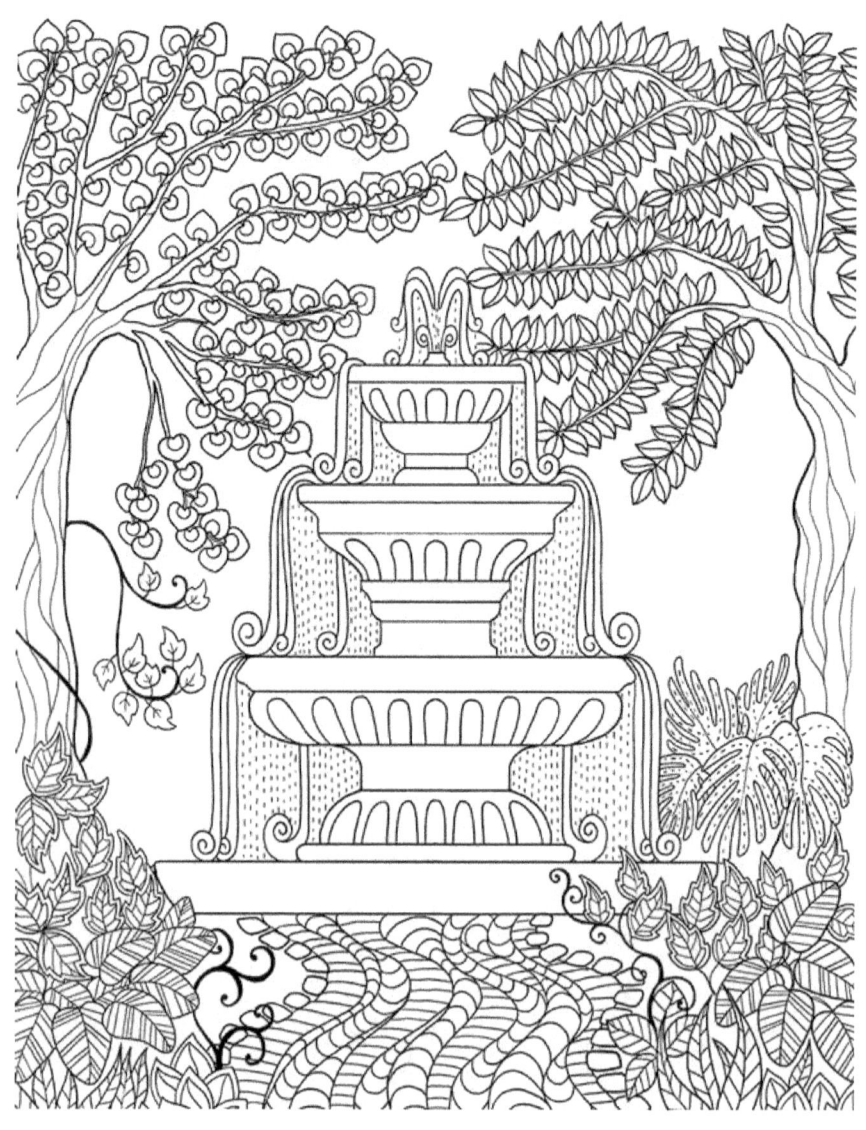

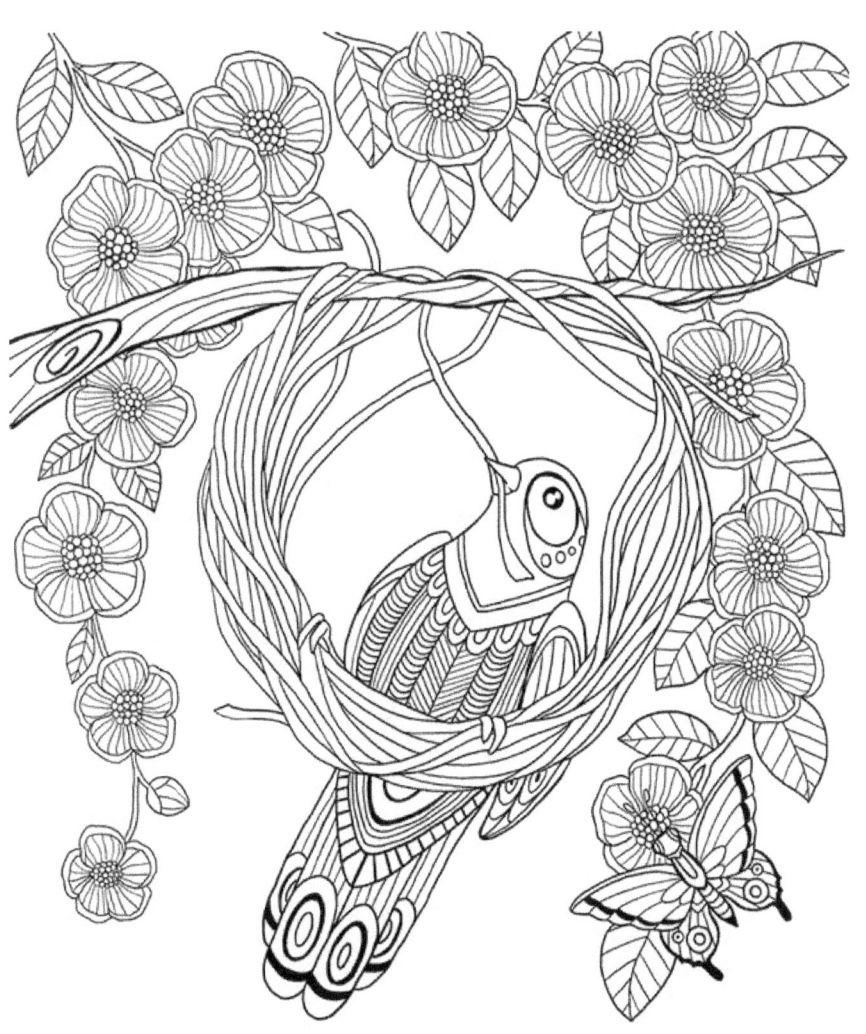

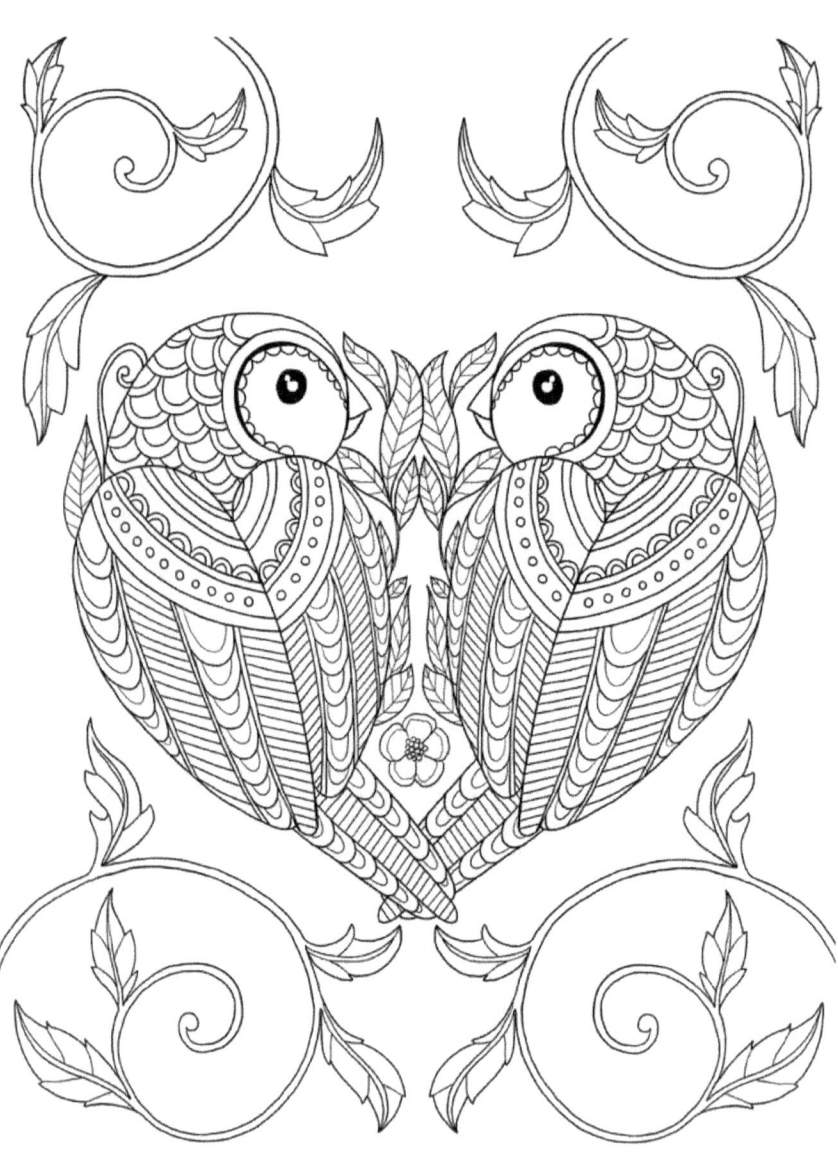

Other Recommended Books on Amazon: (Paperbacks)

Calm Your Mind Coloring Book

Relaxation Time Coloring Book

Mandala Coloring Book

Happy Coloring Books

Tibetan Mandala

www.ingramcontent.com/pod-product-compliance
Lightning Source LLC
Chambersburg PA
CBHW071000180526
45168CB00003B/1229